Property Magic

4th revised and updated edition

How to buy property using other people's time, money and experience

Property Magic

First published in 2008.
Fourth Edition published in September 2012 by

Ecademy Press
48 St Vincent Drive, St⸱ ⸱⸱⸱⸱⸱s, Herts, AL1 5SJ
info@ecademy-press.com
www.ecademy-press.com

Printed and bound by TJ International Ltd, Padstow, Cornwall
Back cover portrait photo courtesy of Clive Reeves.
Cover design and book setting by Neil Coe.

Printed on acid-free paper from managed forests. This book is printed on demand, so no copies will be remaindered or pulped.

ISBN 978-1-908746-47-4

The right of Simon Zutshi to be identified as the author of this work has been inserted in accordance with sections 77 and 78 of the Copyright Designs and Patents Act 1988.

A CIP catalogue record for this book is available from the British Library.

Disclaimer

The information in this book is for educational purposes only. The contents do not constitute financial advice in any way. You should seek independent professional advice before making any investment. Investing in property can be a risky business just like any other investment. Historical growth in property prices does not necessarily mean that prices will increase in the future. Your property may be repossessed if you do not keep up payment on your mortgage.

This book is available online and all good bookstores.

Contents

FOREWORD

Every year I am fortunate enough to be asked to speak at property and wealth events all over the world. As can be expected, the knowledge and successes of the promoters and speakers varies tremendously from event to event. I met Simon Zutshi in October 2008 when I was the guest speaker at his 'Property Magic Live' weekend seminar in London. Not only was the organisation and production first class, but I was struck by Simon's knowledge of the subject, his willingness to share, and his passion for property in general. The event was truly magical. Simon made this possible by surrounding himself with a great team and great participants.

In essence, that is what 'Property Magic' is all about – creating a great team. Property investing can be a lonely pursuit if you are doing it on your own. However, it does not have to be that way. This book explains how to surround yourself with a power team and how to find people who can help you achieve your property investment goals. By leveraging other people's time, money and experience, you can build a solid property portfolio much more quickly and easily than doing so on your own.

Simon is an experienced, successful investor. More importantly for you, however, he is a great mentor and teacher. In this book he simplifies property investing concepts and clearly explains the steps you need to take. This book gives you all the information you need to buy property ethically, well below market value from motivated sellers. Having personally met many of the Property Mastermind delegates who, with Simon's guidance, have taken action and achieved incredible results; I know that if you study and adopt these principles, you too can achieve great success.

It does not matter what is happening to the economy in general, or the property market in particular; now is always a good time to invest in property. This book shows you how to educate yourself, conduct adequate research, buy for the long term,

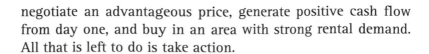

negotiate an advantageous price, generate positive cash flow from day one, and buy in an area with strong rental demand. All that is left to do is take action.

Successful investing,

Dolf de Roos
Phoenix, Arizona

www.dolfderoos.com

Author of the New York Times and international best seller Real Estate Riches

About the author

Simon Zutshi is a financially independent, professional property investor with almost two decades of experience investing in residential property in the UK and overseas.

Simon started investing in 1995 when, as a first time buyer and a recent graduate in debt, he found a strategy to purchase his first property (his home) using none of his own money. By renting out the spare rooms, he was able to cover the mortgage payments and effectively live for free! Caught by the property bug, Simon started to buy more property and, by the age of 32, he was financially independent due to the passive income generated from his property portfolio.

Since an early age, Simon has been interested in the art of magic. He started to perform professionally at the age of 15 and became a member of the world famous Magic Circle in his early 20's. Simon has often said that investing in property draws many parallels with magic, in that once you know the secret, what seemed impossible before is simple to achieve. As with any magic trick, knowing the secret is not always enough, and in order to become truly successful, you must practice and apply your knowledge with skill.

In 2003, Simon founded the Property Investors' Network, which is now a nationwide organisation, to provide a supportive environment for investors to learn more about investing, with the aim of maximising their return and minimising the risks.

Simon now spends most of his time helping and educating other investors by sharing his 'hands on experience' gained over many years as a successful investor. He is one of the few property speakers in the UK who is a member of the Professional Speakers Association. As such, Simon is regularly invited to share his residential property investing strategies at the large property exhibitions and entrepreneurial business conferences in the UK and around the world.

In April 2007 Simon launched his Property Mastermind Programme, which is designed for investors who want to add an extra £1m to their property portfolio and an income of £50,000 in just 12 months. With a limited number of delegates on each programme, it is no surprise that the first Mastermind Programme sold out in less than two hours. Each year there are two programmes, one starting in April and the other in October. To get an inside peek behind the scenes you need to register your interest on the Mastermind website at:

www.Property-Mastermind.com/Magic

www.facebook.com/OfficialSimonZutshi

Understanding the property market

The changing property market

When I first sat down to write Property Magic in December 2007, the market was already changing. The Credit Crunch had started to take effect, property prices were coming down and the Bank of England Interest Base Rate was 5.75%.

I don't think anyone would have been able to predict the changes that have happened since then. Yes, we were expecting the market to slow and show a small correction because it was overheated, but I doubt anyone predicted the dramatic effects this would have on the UK mortgage market and in particular Mortgage Express (MX).

The demise of MX was a real shame for me and everyone else who had been purchasing property No Money Down (NMD) with the aid of the cash purchase (bridging) and same day re-mortgage mainly facilitated by MX.

This strategy was simple and yet very powerful, as anyone could buy a property with absolutely no money required, as long as it was purchased (from a motivated seller) at a genuine 15%+ discount off the open market value. I thought this was incredible, and decided to explain exactly how to do it step by step in Chapter 2 of the original version of Property Magic.

It is rather annoying that two months after publication of the first edition, MX withdrew this facility. I, and those investors in the know, started to use other lenders for this arrangement and found other ways of doing NMD deals, whilst the majority of investors were running around complaining that it was the end of NMD deals. Well it wasn't. We just had to change strategy and adapt. That is what professional investors do.

Although the rest of the book is still valid, Chapter 2 in the first edition is now obsolete, at least for the moment until the strategy is reincarnated in a slightly different form, which I am

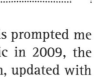

sure will happen at some point in the future. This prompted me to release the second edition of Property Magic in 2009, the third edition in 2010 and now this fourth edition, updated with the latest ways of financing your property portfolio using other people's money. This time, I have made sure it is not quite as specific in talking about particular mortgage products which are still changing on a regular basis.

I thought it would also be useful to include this extra chapter about the property market, as it is important to understand what has happened and what is going to happen, so that anyone who reads this will realise that now really is the very best time to buy residential property in the UK.

Property Cycles

The UK housing market is cyclical just like every other market. It goes up and it goes down. The long term trend in the UK is up, due to the reasons I will outline at the end of this chapter.

The fluctuation in house prices is due to short term changes in supply and demand which is influenced by factors such as interest rates, availability of finance, the media and the effect it has on public sentiment, level of employment and the economy in general.

When investing in property, many people apply the strategy of 'Buy Low and Sell High' which is a strategy borrowed from stock market investing. Whilst there is nothing wrong with the concept behind this strategy, as you will certainly make money if you get it right, I have two fundamental issues with it.

1. It is very hard to establish when a market is truly at the top or bottom, so my view is why guess, when it can be risky if you get it wrong.

2. I much prefer the idea of holding property long term to benefit from the significant capital growth rather than taking short term profits by trading property. There are also tax benefits to holding rather than selling which we will look at in Chapter 1.

What caused prices to fall in 2008?

According to the Barker Report commissioned in 2003 by the UK Government's Treasury Department, there is a shortage of accommodation in the UK. Based on the increasing population, this is only going to get worse. If this is true, then why did the growth in property prices start to slow in 2007, and then fall in 2008? Essentially, this is due to a combination of both a fall in demand and an increased supply of property at the same time, which caused the drop in house prices.

There was a boom in house prices from 2001 to 2007, mainly fuelled by ease of obtaining finance. In this period, many people who were previously unable to get mortgages, were suddenly able to buy their own home, as bad credit was not a problem and even those who were not able to prove an income were able to self certify, which meant they simply declared that they would be able to afford their mortgage payments. As well as the increase in home ownership, there was a raised awareness of making money from property sparked by the plethora of television programs, which bought the idea of property investing to the general public. The increased availability of Buy to Let (BTL) mortgages made it very easy to borrow money to buy investment properties with lenders offering up to 90% Loan To Value (LTV) for Buy to Let mortgages.

Towards the end of this boom period, as prices shot up, investors found that although rents were rising, they were not in line with the increases in property prices. It soon reached a point where investments just did not stack up because the purchase

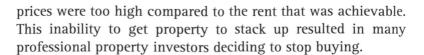

prices were too high compared to the rent that was achievable. This inability to get property to stack up resulted in many professional property investors deciding to stop buying.

The other group of individuals who usually fuel the property market are first time buyers, who also found that they could not afford to purchase at the higher prices, and so also stopped buying. The overheated prices resulted in a decline in demand for property towards the end of 2007 and into 2008.

On the supply side, there were several factors in 2007 that resulted in an increased supply of property for sale in the UK. First of all, in the summer of 2007 the Government introduced Home Information Packs (HIPs) with the purpose of making the buying and selling process more reliable. Anyone selling a property after a certain date would need to pay for a HIP in order to market their property. What actually happened was that people who were thinking about putting their property on the market, rushed to put them on before the deadline and so avoid paying for a HIP. As you can imagine, the market was swamped with properties for sale. The requirement for HIPs has since been dropped by the new Government elected in 2010.

Also in late 2007, the effect of the Credit Crunch had hit the UK. Banks and mortgage lenders suddenly became very fussy about who they would lend money to. This mainly affected home owners with adverse credit, and property investors with properties that did not stack up very well, who had come to the end of fixed rate and discounted mortgages, and then found themselves unable to re-mortgage to cheaper products. Suddenly these people were paying a lot more for their borrowing than before and so many decided to sell their property to get rid of the liability, rather than get into difficulty that could ultimately result in repossession.

When prices get too high, demand will fall off and prices will drop until they reach a level where people start to buy again.

With an average drop of 20% in prices from October 2007 to January 2009, property was suddenly much more affordable. Even though property had come down in value to this more affordable level, most first time buyers and many property investors still did not buy due to the fear of further price falls stimulated by the media.

Having said this, most lenders reported that, on average, UK house prices rose by approximately 8% in 2009. This, of course, is the average growth rate, mainly fuelled by the growth in London, whereas in some places, prices were still falling. A point to note here is that you need to be very careful when looking at average prices because that is exactly what they are: an average across the UK and not necessarily correct for where you may be buying.

Why invest in property now if prices could fall further?

One of the statements that I often hear is "If prices could fall further, then why should I buy now, when I could wait until the market has bottomed out and I can buy at a lower price?" This is a logical statement but is based on the assumption that you buy at full market value. Indeed, if you do pay full market value for your investments, then yes it would make sense to wait until the market bottoms out – that is if you really believe prices could fall further.

However, the strategy of buying at full market value is not the best way to invest, as you will see later in this chapter. You should always buy below market value (BMV) from a motivated seller and that is what this book is all about. If you purchase your investments with a big enough discount, it does not matter if prices fall further, as you will have an equity buffer.

The reality is that when prices are falling and, more importantly, the general public perception is that prices are falling, it will be easier for you to negotiate bigger discounts off the property price. This is because some vendors will be keen to dump their property before it falls much more in value.

Once property prices bottom out and then start to rise again, it is always harder to obtain such large discounts. It is important to understand that there will always be motivated sellers no matter what is happening to the market. However, in a rising market, sellers may be less inclined to accept low offers as they may hang on, in the hope that they will get a higher offer due to the rising market.

What makes prices rise again?

No one can predict accurately when a market will bottom out and start to rise again. I have no idea what will happen in the future and neither does anyone else. What I do know is that in any market there will come a time where prices have fallen to a level so that it is actually cheaper for people to buy and pay a mortgage than to rent. At this point, first time buyers will start to buy again, as long as they can get mortgages.

Whenever prices start to rise, all the amateur investors who have been waiting for the market to bottom out will also start to buy again. History would suggest that it can take several years for prices to rise after a major correction but I think, on this occasion, prices will rise quicker than previously, as there are many more people interested in property investing who will want to make sure they don't miss out on the next rise. These investors will dive back into the market as soon as prices start to rise, which will further fuel the rise. This is as long as these investors can get mortgages to finance their purchases.

The opportunity for you is right now whilst most investors are still waiting. In the 1930s during the Great Depression there were more millionaires made than in any other time in history in the USA, including the dot com boom.

So why wait? This year will be a great year to buy property as long as you follow my five golden rules.

Five Golden Rules of Investing

1. Always buy from motivated sellers

Instead of looking for a property you like and then negotiating with the seller, a smarter strategy is to look for motivated sellers who will be flexible on the price and or the terms of the sale, and then decide if you want to buy that particular property. The amount of discount will vary depending on the motivation of the seller and the general market conditions. In a rising market you may be happy with a 15% to 20% discount. In a falling market you would want a bigger discount of 25% to 40% to give you more of a safety buffer in case prices come down further.

2. Buy in an area with strong rental demand

This is more important than getting a discount! Remember you don't want to be paying for the mortgage on your rental property. That is what you have tenants for. You must make sure there is good rental demand in the area so that if your tenants ever leave, you can quickly find new tenants at the full market rent.

3. Buy for cash flow

Your property should create a monthly positive cash flow for you so that it is an asset rather than a liability. Although we expect property prices to rise in the long term, if you buy your investments 'as if prices will never go up again' you will be forced to only buy properties which give you great cash flow now. Extra cash flow will help you to build up a cash safety buffer, and will help you cover potential rises in interest rates in the future.

4. Invest for the long term buy and hold

Some investors buy and sell property to make a profit. The real profit however is in buying and holding for the long term to benefit from significant capital growth. If you plan to hold for the long term and your property is rented out creating a positive cash flow, you do not mind short term fluctuations in price.

5. Have a cash buffer

The investors who get into difficulty are often the ones who do not have any spare cash to access in case of an emergency. As an investor, you will incur unexpected costs and so you must have some spare cash to cover these instances. The size of this buffer depends on your personal level of risk.

Long term view of property prices

If you consider property investing as a long term investment, then short term price fluctuations should not really be of concern as long as you have carefully followed my Five Golden Rules of Investing.

Despite these occasional short term fluctuations in the UK property market, the long term trend is up, due to the fundamental reason that demand is greater than supply.

We live on a very popular island with limited space and an increasing population. A significant part of the countryside is Green Belt and so protected from development and yet demand for accommodation continues to increase due to easier immigration, increasing divorce rates and changing social demographic trends, such as more young people going to university. The demand for accommodation is ever-increasing. The number of new homes being built each year slowed dramatically due to the downturn in the market in 2008.

In the 2003 Barker Report, mentioned earlier in this chapter, the conclusion was that if the housing trends at the time continued, by the year 2009 there would not be enough homes in the UK. By 2020 we would have a shortfall of three million homes. What do you think this will do to house prices and the demand for rental accommodation? Over the last 60 years, property prices in the UK have, on average, doubled every seven to nine years. Remember this is an average, it does not happen EVERY seven to nine years. I believe we could see prices double again in the next 10 years but we shall have to wait and see.

Risks of investing

A final word of caution before we start. Is it possible to lose money in property? Yes, of course it is. There are risks associated with anything you do in life. However, if you educate yourself and do your research you can mitigate many of the risks that you may encounter.

There is one particular risk that I want to mention here as I believe it may cause a problem for many investors in the future. That risk is the possibility of very high interest rates. As a direct result of all the money that has been printed in the UK and around the world, I am sure we will see some high inflation over the next few years. The Bank of England will probably use increased interest rates as a tool to control inflation.

It is worth noting here that inflation can be a good thing for us as property investors. Inflation means that the cost of living goes up, which also means the value of our properties rises as does the cost of renting a property, which means we receive more rental income. If we use interest-only mortgages on our investments, although the amount we own on each property remains the same cash amount, the true value of this debt is eroded over time thanks to inflation.

I can't give you financial advice and this book is meant to be purely educational but I will share my personal anti-inflationary strategy. On all the new mortgages I take out and any re-mortgages, I am fixing my interest rate for as long as possible, in an attempt to safeguard against high unaffordable interest rates over the next few years.

You should seek the advice of a qualified independent financial advisor and ask them their view on what could happen to interest rates over the next few years.

Don't allow the fear of potential high interest rates to be another reason not to invest. There are ways of controlling property without even having a mortgage, that I will share later in this book.

Chapter 1:

You should be investing in property

You need to provide for your future

It's a sad fact that 98% of the population will die poor! As a nation we are all living longer, and that means we need more money to support us into our old age. In my opinion, it is unlikely that the state will be able to afford to support us. Most people can't rely on their company pension scheme. What this means for you is that unless you do something about it now, you will either have to keep working beyond the normal retirement age or accept a lower standard of living in your old age. That is unless you do something about it, which is probably why you are reading this book.

You have several options open to you:

1. You could start a business to generate some extra income.

2. You could invest in the stock market.

3. You could invest in property.

Personally I have done all three and I can confidently say that investing in property is far easier, safer and can give a much better return than the other two options.

Property is one of the best investments you can make

People will always need somewhere to live. Here in the UK, we live on a popular island where the demand for accommodation is increasing. This means that, in the long term, prices should continue to increase. Whilst this is a reassuring fact, it is not actually the biggest benefit of investing in property over any other asset.

The main benefit of investing in property is the ability to invest using other people's money. The use of this gearing (or leverage) makes property investment stand head and shoulders above all other possible investments. Let's say you have a lump sum of £30,000 to invest. If you chose to put the money into the stock market you could buy £30,000 worth of shares. If you selected your shares wisely and the company performed at the average growth rate of the stock market, which is a compound rate of 12% a year, then your investment of £30,000 would double to about £60,000 in just over five years time. This would be a 100% return on your investment in five years. That's not bad – a rate of about 20% per year, thanks to the compounding. I think most people would invest more in the stock market at that kind of return, if only it was that easy to find good stock.

If you took the same £30,000 and invested it in property rather than shares, you would be able to purchase a £100,000 investment. This is, of course, possible through gearing and the use of other people's money. To buy an investment property, currently you need a 25% deposit, thus to purchase the £100,000 property you would need a deposit of £25,000 and the balance of £75,000 would come from the 75% LTV, buy to let mortgage. Out of your £30,000 lump sum you would still have £5,000 left which would cover your purchase costs and maybe some furniture.

On Average (over the last 60 years) property prices usually grow at about 9% per annum, but for this example just to compare like with like, let's say that it grows at the same rate as the stock market and so use a growth rate of 12% per annum. (This was the average rate at which property prices grew from 2001 to 2007 but they were years of exceptional growth).

If your investment property were to increase in value at 12% per year, just like the shares, it would also double in value in the same time period. The value of your property will have increased from £100,000 to £200,000. However, you will have benefited from an increase in equity of £100,000 from your initial investment of just £30,000, which means that you will have had a 333% return on your investment (ROI). I am not aware of any other way to generate this kind of return safely on your investment.

In reality, with an average growth rate of 9% per year it might take eight years for your property to double in value. So 333% in eight years is still an average of 41.6% per year ROI. That is still a very strong return. Even at a very conservative growth rate of just 5% per annum, it would take 14 years for your property to double in value, giving you an average ROI of 23.8% per year. This is still more than you could make if your money was in a bank.

These rates of ROI are based on you putting in a 25% deposit. However, if you reduce the amount of deposit you put into the property your ROI shoots up. Later in this book, I will share with you how to buy property and rapidly recycle the deposit, so that you have no money left in the deal which means that you have an infinite ROI.

If you are using other people's money in the form of a mortgage, there is, of course, a cost to doing this. You will have to pay interest on the borrowed money. But here is the really clever part. You don't personally have to pay for the cost of borrowing, your tenant does! You don't live in the property and so you can let it out to someone else who pays you rent which you use to cover all of the holding costs, such as mortgage interest, insurance, management fees etc. This means that once you have an investment property, you can benefit from the long term growth without having to make short term contributions. It is like having someone else make contributions for you into your pension fund. This is as long as you make sure you buy a property in an area with strong rental demand which stacks up, i.e. where the rental income covers all of the monthly expenses.

It is easy to understand why some people believe that you get a better return in the stock market than you do in property. The historical growth rate of the stock market has been an average of 12% per annum whereas the UK property market has only grown at a lower average rate of 9% per annum. Based on this one factor, many people assume that they get a better return in the stock market. They completely miss the point about gearing. Your property investment may well increase in value at a slower rate, but you get a better ROI as the growth is actually on a far larger investment, thanks to the fact that you can borrow money.

But is property really a safe investment? If you ask your bank for a loan, they will ask you why you want the money. If you tell them that you want the money to buy shares, they will tell you that they cannot help you. However, if you tell them you want to buy a property they will invite you in to have a chat about it. This is because they know that property is a safe long term investment. Not the case with stocks and shares.

Now is a fantastic time to buy property as long as you know what you are doing. As you'll see later in this book, there are plenty of motivated sellers who will sell you their property for less than it is worth. If you buy at enough of a discount and recycle your deposit, then there that there is no limit to the amount of property you can buy.

With this in mind, why wouldn't you buy as much property as you can? Property can do so much for you. If you want, property can just generate some extra cash for you every month to help pay the bills or improve your lifestyle. If you buy enough of the right type of property, you can even generate enough passive income every month to replace your salary, which means that you will be financially independent and you won't need to work! If you no longer need to work, trading your time for money, you are free to do whatever you want with your time. It does take some effort and time to get to that financially free situation, but it is perfectly possible. If you are fortunate enough to have a great job which you really enjoy and which pays you well, you may not want to give up work and that's fine, but property will help you build a solid pension for your future. Finally, you may want to invest for the future of your family, to leave a legacy to your loved ones. Whatever your reasons, I think it is important to be clear in your own mind why you want to invest in property. Take a moment now to consider what you would like your property portfolio to do for you.

Why don't more people invest in property?

Most people recognise that investing in property is probably the best investment they can make, but unfortunately they don't do it. Something prevents them from taking the necessary action. What about you? Have you taken as much action as you should? Let's consider for a moment a few of the challenges that people face when thinking about investing in property.

Fear: We have all heard horror stories of people who have lost money when investing in property; of people who have had nightmare tenants. It is true, there can be problems associated with property investing but, in reality, most problems can be mitigated. It is only natural that people feel the fear and often it can paralyse people into a state of indecision. They are not sure what to do, so they do nothing.

Ignorance: Most people don't really understand what property can do for them and they are ignorant of why it is such a good investment. People don't bother to educate themselves because they don't know what they don't know. Or even worse, they think they know but actually they don't know. Some of the hardest people for me to educate are those who already have one or two investment properties and they think they know it all.

Lack of knowledge: There are people who really want to invest in property but have no idea of how or where to start. When I first started investing in property, there were a few books about property investing, but that was it. I had to learn the hard way by trial and error. Today it is easy for you to learn from other successful investors through books, DVDs, seminars and even coaching and mentoring. There is no excuse for not knowing what to do. The first problem is that often people don't know what they don't know! The second problem is often that people are not prepared to invest in their own education. Investing in yourself is probably the best investment you will ever make, even better than property!

Lack of time: We are all busy and most people feel they don't have enough time to do everything they would like to do. Property investing is often one of those things that people know they should do, but they feel that they just don't have the time for. The irony is that if you invest just some of your time in building your property portfolio now, you will become financially independent in the future, which means that you can retire early and spend all of your time doing whatever you want to do, since you will not need to work for a living. We all have the same amount of time. It's a matter of how you decide to spend your time or invest your time.

Lack of money: This is one of the biggest barriers to property investing as most people are conditioned to believe that you need to have money to invest in property. However, if you know the correct strategy, you don't need much of your own money to invest in property. These strategies will be explained in full later in this book.

Impatience: In today's society many people have a very short term view. If they don't get instant results they give up very easily. This can be a problem with property investing, which is a long-term investment and benefits come from a buy and hold strategy. You can make good cash flow from property right now, but the real value is in the long-term capital growth.

Tax: Incredibly, I've actually heard some people say that they don't want to invest in property because they will have to pay tax. This is absolutely crazy. You only have to pay tax when you make money, so surely having to pay lots of tax means you're making lots of money. Isn't that a good thing? The other important factor to consider here is that rich people usually don't pay very much tax. This is because rich people can afford to get good tax advice, which means that although they will pay some tax, generally they will pay fewer pence in the pound in tax than someone who is earning less money and cannot afford the right tax advice. Later in this book you will learn how to make tax-free money from your property, minimise your income tax and minimise the inheritance tax due on your estate.

Just for a moment I would like you to consider which of these factors may have limited you in the past, prevented you from investing in property and taking action to secure your financial future. How much has it cost you in lost opportunity to allow these concerns and fears to get in your way? I suppose the fact that you are reading this book means you have decided to do something about it. I congratulate you on this decision, and look forward to accompanying you on your journey of discovery about property investment.

So what is your strategy?

When I first started to invest in property, I didn't have a strategy. I just knew that property was a good investment and so I started to buy and I seem to have muddled through somehow. I think many people start like this, but if I was starting to invest now, I would certainly be very clear and focused on my strategy. You need to work out what you want property to do for you. Some property will give you strong capital growth, some investments will give you great cash flow and occasionally if you are lucky you might get both. You need to think about what is important to you. What you ultimately want to achieve will shape your strategy, which will influence the type of property you purchase.

A vital part of your strategy planning is to consider your exit strategy. This will have a big effect on the structure within which you buy property, the type of property you buy, and maybe even the way you finance it.

Have you considered your exit strategy?

I have always understood that historically, on average, property prices in the UK double every seven to nine years. Based on this understanding, my initial exit strategy was very simple.

The idea was to start buying investment property where the rent would more than cover the costs and so give me a positive cash flow. I was quite successful at this, so that by the age of 32 I was financially independent, due to the income from my rental properties. I thought I would stop buying at some point and then just wait for my portfolio to double in value. Once the portfolio had doubled in value I was planning to sell half of the properties and use the proceeds from the sale to pay off all of the mortgages on the remaining half of my portfolio. I would then own the remaining properties outright and so would make a great positive cash flow, since I would have no mortgages to pay but would still receive the rental income from them. This seemed like common sense to me and I know that many investors have an exit strategy similar to this.

Consider a numerical example of this: Assume that you were able to buy 10 properties over a few years. If the average value of each property was £100,000 then the total value of your portfolio would be £1m. There would probably be mortgages on your portfolio of at least 75% LTV, which would equate to £750,000 of debt. Conservatively, it could take at least 10 years for the property market to double in value again. In that time, your 10 properties would each have doubled in value from £100,000 to £200,000, making your total portfolio of 10 properties worth £2m. At this point, if you were to sell half of your portfolio you would raise £1m from the sale before tax and sales costs. By utilising your various capital gains allowances, you could end up with net revenue sufficient to completely clear the original £750,000 of debt. This would leave you with five properties valued at £200,000 each with no debt. Would you be happy with a £1m debt-free property portfolio?

This seemed like a great idea to me. However, after seeking expert tax advice, I realised that this was not a very tax-efficient strategy for three main reasons:

1. You would have to pay Capital Gains Tax (CGT) on all the properties that were sold. There are ways of minimising your CGT but, in reality, if you are selling half of your portfolio, even if you stagger it over a number of years there will be some CGT to pay.

2. Using the proceeds of the sales to repay all of the mortgages on the properties, you would have no interest to offset against rental income. This means that you would pay Income Tax (IT) on all of your rental income.

3. But the final tax problem is Inheritance Tax (IHT). If you clear all your debts and own your properties outright, there will be a large IHT liability in the future on your estate.

Although in essence this is a good strategy, it is not very tax-efficient as you will have to pay lots of CGT, IT and IHT. I understand the importance of paying tax and contributing to society but why pay more tax than you have to if there is an alternative, more tax-efficient strategy?

I decided to change my strategy as follows: Instead of selling half of my portfolio, and using the sales proceeds to clear the mortgage debt, I have decided to keep all of the property and its associated debt forever! I am re-mortgaging the property as it increases in value and rental income will allow. As you will already know, the cash generated from a re-mortgage is tax-free because it is debt. There are three distinct tax advantages for us with this new exit strategy:

1. If you don't sell, you never pay CGT. At death, any CGT liability on your property portfolio is wiped out.

2. You will still have mortgage interest payments, which can be offset against your rental income, reducing your IT liability.

3. By constantly re-mortgaging your property and removing equity, you will be increasing your level of debt, which at the same time will reduce your net assets and so reduce potential IHT liability on your estate.

Back to the numerical example:

Your 10 properties have each doubled in value from £100,000 to £200,000 in 10 years, so that the total value of your portfolio is now £2m. The initial borrowing was £750,000 (75% LTV). If you increase the borrowing over the 10 year period by re-mortgaging each property at an appropriate time, then you would be able to withdraw a substantial amount of cash, tax-free, out of your portfolio.

As you re-mortgage your portfolio over time, if you were to maintain the level of borrowing at 75% LTV, you would be able to borrow up to £1.5m against the portfolio value of £2m. With your original mortgages of just £750,000, this would be an increase in borrowing of £750,000 that you had taken out of your portfolio over a 10-year period. This works out to an average of £75,000 each year, tax-free money in your pocket. Would that help your lifestyle?

There are two drawbacks to this strategy:

1. If you ever had to sell a property from which you have withdrawn substantial amounts of cash as the value had increased over time, it is possible that the CGT payable on the property may well be more than the profits generated from the sale of that property. It is important to make sure that you can hold onto these properties for life.

2. At the time of writing, the Inland Revenue will only allow you to offset mortgage interest against rental income on borrowing up to the value of the property at the time at which you first rent it out. This means that you may not get tax relief on all of the increased interest you have to pay, as a result of having re-mortgaged the property. In that case it would be worth putting aside some of the tax-free cash generated from the re-mortgage to cover these interest payments in the future.

I have adapted my exit strategy to this far more tax-efficient model. This illustration is meant for educational purposes only. I recommend you consult a qualified tax expert to give you advice based on your personal circumstances. A word of caution here: most supposed tax experts don't understand property investing. So, as is always the case, you need to make sure the expert from whom you are seeking advice really understands property investing and ideally will also be an investor themselves, so that they understand exactly what you are aiming to achieve. Over the years, I have met several qualified and regulated IFAs (Independent Financial Advisors) who know absolutely nothing about property investing and so advise their clients not to invest in property. This is a real shame as their clients have missed out on significant capital value appreciation due to the lack of knowledge of the so-called professional advisor.

Buy as an individual or company?

This is often a question that I am asked. As mentioned above, I am not qualified to give you tax advice and it does depend on your personal circumstances. However, in general if you want to buy and hold property for the long term and use the equity release strategy described, then buying as an individual would make more sense. And also it is easier to get mortgages as an individual than as a company. If you want to trade property short term then a company structure may be more tax efficient.

You can do it - all you need is the right system

The good news is that anybody can invest in property. Property investment is like magic in that it is quite simple when you know how to do it. But the results that you can achieve are incredible, just like magic. The purpose of this book is to show you not only what you can do, but how you can do it. Even better than that, you don't have to do it all on your own. The Mastermind principle that I will share with you later in this book will show you how you can build your property portfolio using other people's time, money, knowledge and expertise.

The main focus of this book is how you can buy property from motivated sellers. By purchasing below market value you lock in profit on the day you buy, rather than having to wait for the capital appreciation. You also give yourself a buffer against falls in the property value.

The information is all here for you. All you need to do is to put it into action. Unfortunately, this is where most people fail. They know what they need to do, they know they should do it, but they fail to take the necessary action. I believe this is because they don't have the right mindset. You can have all the strategies in the world but if you don't have the correct attitude and mindset they will not really work for you. So in addition to showing you what to do, I am going to spend a good section of this book helping you to work on your mindset.

To get the most out of this book, I recommend you read it from front to back, and then read it again, and finally use it as a reference to dip in and out of. This is your book, so please write in it and make notes as and when you feel necessary.

Chapter 2:

You can buy property with none of your own money.

There is a common belief that you need to have a lot of money to be able to invest in property. Whilst it is true that having money will make it much easier to invest, it is possible to invest without using any of your own money.

I meet investors all the time who have stopped buying because they have run out of deposits. They all seem to have a similar story. When they first realised how powerful property investing could be for them and for their financial future, they used all the money they could, from savings, inheritance or released equity from their home, to buy as many buy to let (BTL) investment properties as possible.

They used the maximum LTV borrowing so that they could make the most of their deposit money and spread it across as many BTL properties as possible. The problem that all investors run into is that no matter how much money they have for deposits, at some point they will run out, and at this point most people stop because they think they can't afford to buy any more investment properties.

Then most investors sit back and wait. They wait until property prices have risen enough such that they can re-mortgage their investments to pull out some cash which can then be recycled as deposits to buy even more properties and so the cycle continues. This is a great strategy to build your portfolio over the long term.

The obvious problem is that this is a long term strategy and you have to wait for the sufficient capital appreciation of the properties to be able to pull out money to fund your next purchase.

There is a two-part solution to this particular problem: Firstly, rather than using your own money for deposits, use other people's money instead, and secondly reduce the amount of time required until there's sufficient equity in the property to refinance. This can be done by buying the property significantly

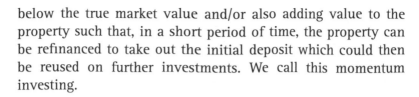

below the true market value and/or also adding value to the property such that, in a short period of time, the property can be refinanced to take out the initial deposit which could then be reused on further investments. We call this momentum investing.

In this chapter we are going to explore this solution to show you how you can buy as many properties as you like using other people's money. But first let's make sure you understand some of the basics related to financing your property investments.

Residential mortgages

When you buy your own home you take out a standard residential mortgage which generally requires a deposit of typically 10% to 15%. Prior to the Credit Crunch at the end of 2007, in some circumstances you wouldn't need any deposit at all because the bank would lend you 100% of the value of the property if you had a good enough income. Your personal credit score and income are very important.

There were some lenders who would even lend as much as 130% of the value of the property. If you were buying your home for £100,000 they would actually lend you £130,000 so you could use the extra 30% to do whatever you wanted.

Some smart people took that extra 30% and used it for a deposit to buy a second property which they could rent out. Many not so wise people enjoyed that money, went on holiday, purchased cars, etc. and they found themselves in a bit of a problem a few years later when they wanted to sell the house and move on; they found the debt was far higher than the value of the property. This is one of the factors that helped cause the Credit Crunch in the first place. Understandably, banks are far more cautious now.

Buy To Let mortgages

When you buy a property that is not your own home, you need a specialist BTL mortgage where the lender is aware that you will not be living there, but instead letting it out to tenants who will pay you rent.

The amount of mortgage you can obtain will vary depending on the mortgage market conditions. Most of my BTL properties I have purchased with 85% LTV mortgages and even up to 90% LTV mortgages in some circumstances when the market was booming.

With the Credit Crunch, the mortgage market changed radically and the availability of investment mortgages reduced drastically as did the LTV that lenders were prepared to lend against BTL investments. With maximum lending of 75% LTV, investors would need a 25% deposit. The maximum LTV available for BTL mortgages will naturally increase as the market recovers and the banks regain confidence.

The difference between mortgages and re-mortgages

Although it may sound obvious, this is a key concept that many investors find very difficult to comprehend when they first learn about these creative strategies.

Normally, when you buy a property initially you get a mortgage. If you own a property that you refinance it's called a re-mortgage. There is a fundamental difference between a mortgage and a re-mortgage. When you buy a property, the mortgage is generally based on the purchase price of the property or the value, whichever is lower. However, a re-mortgage is based on the value of the property and the purchase price is not so important.

Let me elaborate. Let's say you own a property which you want to refinance. You arrange for a re-mortgage of the property. The mortgage lender you choose would instruct a surveyor to conduct a valuation of the property. The surveyor will assess how much the property is worth but very rarely will ask you about the purchase price, because as it is a re-mortgage it doesn't really matter. It is all based on the value of the property. If the property was worth £120,000, the lender would probably give you a loan of 75% of the value, which in this case would be a loan of £90,000. A point to note here is that most lenders in the UK will want you to own the property for six months before you are able to re-mortgage it.

Now let's assume that you don't own this particular property but you are buying it at full market value. You would be buying the property for £120,000. The surveyor would come round to value the property and, on this occasion as it is a mortgage, they would be interested in how much you purchase the property for and they would base the loan on that purchase price. A 75% LTV mortgage would mean that you could get a loan of £90,000, which is 75% of the purchase price. As usual with most purchases, you will be required to put in a 25% deposit, which in this case would be £30,000; nothing unusual about this so far.

Taking this example one stage further, let's say that although the house is worth £120,000, the motivated seller, who needs to sell their house quickly, has agreed to sell it to you for just £88,000. The surveyor would be sent to the property to conduct a valuation on behalf of your mortgage lender. Once the surveyor discovers how much you are paying for it, the lender would give you a mortgage based on that purchase price of £88,000. A typical 75% mortgage would give you a loan of £66,000 even though the property is worth £120,000. Remember, you would only get a mortgage of £66,000 because the mortgage is based on the purchase price not the value. This is unfortunate as we have seen previously that if you already owned this property and were to re-mortgage it, you would be able to get a loan of £90,000 as this would be 75% of the value.

Momentum Investing

One way to purchase this investment would be to buy the property at the agreed £88,000 with an £66,000 mortgage and a £22,000 deposit. Once you have owned the property for six months, you could refinance it and, based on the value of £120,000, you could apply for a re-mortgage of £90,000. This means you would get back your £22,000 deposit plus an extra £2,000, which may cover some of your purchase costs. This is certainly one way to do it.

The main problem is that you tie up the deposit for six months until you can re-mortgage the property and you also have increased costs due to having two surveys, two sets of legal costs and potentially two arrangement fees on the finance.

Another potential issue when you come to remortgage is that you may struggle to prove the true value at £120k if you originally purchased it just six months previously for £88k. To overcome this it can be useful to obtain an independent RICS (Royal institute of Chartered surveyors) valuation BEFORE you purchase it to show the true value of £120k, and take some pictures before and after any work you do to demonstrate that you have added value.

Creative ways to buy property

As a sophisticated investor you need to keep up to date with the market and how it is changing. There will always be creative ways to buy property but they will change over time.

The creative method described in the first edition of Property Magic was as follows: You buy the property at the discounted rate for cash. Once you are the owner, you can re-mortgage the property on the same day with a loan based on the true value. In this example, you would buy the property for £88,000 and arrange a re-mortgage for £90,000, thus covering the entire purchase price and giving you £2,000 to cover your purchase costs. Purchasing the property in this manner means that you have acquired a property with £30,000 of equity, using none of your own money.

The ways of buying with none of your own money are described later in this chapter but before we consider these, let's just look at a case study of the very first deal "No Money Down" (NMD) deal I did back in 2006. The discount I achieved effectively gave me the equity for the deposit.

It is worth noting here that the UK Government introduced some new legislation on 1st July 2009 regarding Sale and Rent Back (SARB) which means that investors looking to do this kind of deal need to be regulated by the Financial Services Authority. You can still buy property NMD from motivated sellers but just cannot allow them to rent back the property from you. I think this will result in more properties being repossessed from people who could have been helped by investors like you and me, but we will have to wait and see.

CASE STUDY: My first NMD purchase

My first NMD property purchase was in Nottingham. The owner of this property (let's call him Bob) had been made redundant and had slipped behind with the mortgage payments on his home. Bob also had an unsecured loan with the bank. Bob was paying a high rate of interest and just could not keep up with repayments, and so slipped behind to the point that, when I first met him, Bob was about a month away from having his property repossessed.

I initially spoke to Bob on the telephone and agreed to go and have a look at the property and see if I could help him. I asked Bob what he wanted in return for his property. He made it clear that all he really wanted was to pay off all of the debts and to have £2,000 left in his hand, and he wanted to rent back the property long term at an affordable rent.

His mortgage was £56,000 and his bank loan was £6,000. This meant that I was able to purchase the property for £64,000, which included the £2,000 Bob wanted in his hand. We both knew that this price was significantly below the true market value which was about £90,000.

To be honest, I couldn't quite understand why Bob was prepared to sell his property at such a discounted price. However, Bob had considered all the other options and selling the house was really the only thing he could do. He also wanted to be able to stay in the house as he had lived there for nearly 20 years. I asked Bob what he could afford to pay in terms of rent, to which he replied that he could afford about £400 a month. The average market rent for this type of property in the area was more like £475 per month but as he was selling the property to me at a discount I agreed to rent the property back to him at the discounted rent for as long as he wanted.

Having agreed the deal, I left Bob's house and immediately phoned my mortgage broker to instruct him to apply for the re-mortgage and survey on the property. Next I called my solicitor and instructed her to carry out the searches on the property. Finally I also called the second solicitor and asked them to contact Bob to represent him in the sale of the property.

Based on my research, I estimated the property was worth

between £90,000 and £100,000. I asked my mortgage broker to put a value of £95,000 on the re-mortgage application form. The lender's surveyor visited the property to carry out his valuation and agreed that the value of the property was £95,000. Based on the value of £95,000, the lender was prepared to give me an 85% re-mortgage equivalent to £80,750. As you can see, the re-mortgage loan was much greater than the purchase price. This meant that I would be getting some tax-free cash out of the deal.

On the completion day, my solicitor used £68,500 in bridging to purchase the property. This covered the £64,000 required for the actual purchase and £4,500 to cover all of the purchase costs, which included the solicitors' fees on both sides, the cost of the bridging, and the finder's fee for the property. Once the property was in my name, the solicitor was able to use the funds from the re-mortgage to pay back the bridging and the balance of approximately £12,000 was sent to me. This meant that on my very first BMV purchase, I was able to pull £12,000 tax-free cash out of the deal and end up with a property worth £95,000 with £14,250 equity in it, and a tenant in the property from day one who, although paying slightly less than the market rent, was paying enough to cover all the monthly costs.

At the time, I was able to get an 85% LTV re-mortgage but even with one at 75% LTV I would have still walked out with £2,750 in tax-free cash and had a mortgage of £71,250 and equity of £23,750. Still a great deal!

Is it easy to find this kind of deal?

That was a pretty good first deal. You may like to know how I found that deal in the first place. Well, I didn't find it myself. I purchased the lead from another investor who had found Bob, but didn't want to go ahead with the purchase because the property was out of his area and not the kind of property he would normally buy. I paid 2% (of the purchase price) plus VAT for the lead. I would be happy to buy that kind of lead anytime. Who wouldn't?

I sometimes hear about other investors complaining that there is too much competition in the market for these below market value properties. Whilst I agree that there are apparently lots of investors looking for these deals, I would also argue that most of the investors in the market are amateurs and just do not know how to do these deals properly. It's not just about finding the deal. You need to be able to build a good relationship with the seller so that they work with you, rather than your competition. I discovered that I wasn't the first investor to visit Bob in his home. While I was chatting with him, Bob told me that another company had been round to the property two weeks earlier but had not got back to him. I expressed my surprise at this and reassured Bob that if he worked with me, I would deal with his property sale in a fast and professional manner. I was able to build sufficient rapport with Bob such that he decided to work with me, instead of the other company that had been messing him around. It just goes to show that you need to be quick if you want to buy this kind of property. It is also vital that you are professional and ethical, but more on that in Chapter 4.

The best source of deposit finance

First of all you need to look at your own resources. Do you have any savings in the bank or equity in any property that you could release to be used for deposits? Many people don't like the idea of using equity in their own home to invest as they are worried about the risks!

If this is how you feel, I would like you to think again. Here is a simple strategy for you to pay off your home mortgage and build a property portfolio in just eight to ten years. It's a very safe, slow strategy.

For the sake of this example, let's assume you've got some equity in your home. In fact, for many years you have been working hard to pay off your home mortgage. Please note that if you are only ever going to have one property (the home you live in) then it is a very good idea to pay off your home mortgage as quickly as you possibly can. By paying off your home mortgage you will be reducing one of your biggest outgoing expenses and you will reach financial independence far more quickly. However, investors think differently about this.

For most people, their home is the biggest asset they will ever own. Many people are content to pay off the mortgage, happy in the knowledge that, over time, the value of their asset will increase. If your home is worth £200,000 now then you could just sit back and relax and in 10 years time your property will probably double in value to £400,000. How would that make you feel?

Does this mean you are financially better off? Well, if your house is worth £400,000 you may feel much better than when it was worth £200,000. But in reality you are no better off. You see, all the other properties will also have gone up in value. If you wanted to move from your existing house to a similar size house, that would also cost you £400,000. In real terms you've had no net gain. And for you to benefit from that increase in value you would have to sell the house and downsize to a smaller, cheaper property or move to a cheaper area which is what many people do when they retire.

Investors recognise that it's beneficial to have more than one property because they can profit from the increased capital value of their entire property portfolio, especially if they've used other people's money to buy that portfolio.

Consider this alternative strategy. Instead of trying to pay off their own home as quickly as possible, investors will do the opposite! They will use as much equity as they can from their existing properties to buy more to expand the portfolio.

Remember, in this example we are going to assume you've got £200,000 of equity in your own home and let's say you could release up to 80% of the value of that equity, which means that you would be able to release £160,000 to use as seed capital for your deposits.

To keep the example simple we will assume the BTL properties you would purchase are worth about £100,000 in today's market.

If you were to use 75% LTV mortgages, that means you could get a £75,000 BTL mortgage on each investment property and you would be required to put in a £25,000 deposit.

With seed capital of £160,000, you would have deposits for six investment properties (6 x £25,000 = £150,000) and you would have £10,000 left over to cover your purchasing costs such as solicitor's and surveyor's fees.

You would then be the proud owner of a property portfolio containing your own home (worth £200,000) and six investments at £100,000 each (6 x £100,000) with a total value of £800,000.

Don't forget that you will also have some debt! There is the £160,000 mortgage from your own home, and you also have six BTL mortgages of £75,000 (6 x £75,000 = £450,000) which means your total debt is £610,000. That might feel like a lot of debt and it might scare you, but the great thing is you are not going to be covering the cost of that debt. The tenants in your rental properties should be covering the cost of that borrowing.

Having done the initial hard work finding and buying the right six properties, you sit back and wait! If property prices were to double on average in the next 10 years, your total portfolio would increase in value from £800,000 to £1.6m.

Your outstanding debt which was taken out as interest-only mortgages is still only £610,000. That means you have almost £1m of equity – that's quite a good lump of equity to have.

At some point in the future you would want to pay off the mortgage on your own home. Each of the investment properties would be worth £200,000 with a BTL mortgage of just £75,000. What you could do is to re-mortgage some or all of those investment properties to take out, let's say, £27,000 from each property. That would give you £160,000 in cash which you could use to clear all of the debt on your own home and you would still have the six investment properties giving you a rental income and almost £1m in equity.

Alternative sources of deposit finance

If you do not have any equity available then think about everyone you know who may have some. I am sure you have family and friends who have plenty of equity and would like to invest in property but have no idea how to do it. You could joint venture with them whereby you put in the time and effort and they provide the seed capital for deposits.

Maybe you have a business that has retained profits. Rather than leaving the money in the bank, could you use a director's loan from your business and pay interest to you business for the loan.

Where else could you borrow money from? Could you take out a private loan? I have even purchased property using credit card cheques for the deposit, although this is an advanced strategy and you need to be very careful that you have a clear exit strategy. I would not recommend this.

Do you have any family from whom you will eventually inherit some money? Would it be possible to get some of that money in advance? If they give you some money and then live for at least another seven years, the gift would be considered to be outside of their estate and so would avoid any IHT liability. The other main benefit is that they see you prospering from their gift while they are still alive. We call this giving with warm hands!

Maybe you know some other investors with whom you can do joint ventures. We talk more about this in Chapter 7.

Or finally, how about the seller of the property that you want to purchase? What are they going to do with the proceeds of the sale? If they are downsizing do they need all of the money? If they are just going to put the money in their bank, then maybe you can give them a better return on investment.

There are many different ways to find the deposits. The key here is to remember that you want to use as little of your own money as possible.

The next step

Once you have sourced the deposit finance, you need to focus on finding motivated sellers who will sell their property to you for less than the true market value.

By purchasing at a significant discount (and adding value where possible) you should be able to refinance the property quickly or get a further advance to pull out the deposit and use it on the next purchase, thus building a portfolio with No Money Left In (NMLI).

The good news is that there are motivated sellers everywhere; You just need to know where and how to find them and, more importantly, how to help them solve their problems which is exactly what we will cover in the next two chapters.

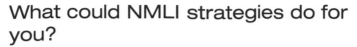

What could NMLI strategies do for you?

Using these strategies, there is no limit to the number of properties you can buy. All you need to do is to find the motivated sellers, know how to deal with them and take action to make sure the deal happens. How many properties are you going to buy over the next 12 months?

The average property value in the UK is about £160,000. If you were to obtain a 25% discount on this value of property, you would get £40,000 of equity each time you buy a property.

If you bought one property a month, after 12 month's you would have £1.92m worth of property with £480,000 of equity; that's very good, but let's consider what happens in ten years time when those properties may well have doubled in value. Your £1.92m of property will be worth something like £3.84m. The equity in your property portfolio will be worth £2.4m. Would that be enough money to support you and your family in your retirement?

Let me just clarify that all you would be doing is buying one property each month for 12 months. That's it! I am not talking about working for 10 years. I am talking about working smart for just one year then you just sit back and wait while the value of your properties increases with time. If you put your mind to it, do you think you could do it?

Chapter 3:

There are plenty of
motivated sellers
who will sell you
their property for
less than it is worth.

Why would someone sell their property below market value?

If you've ever sold a property, I am sure you probably wanted to achieve the highest possible sale price. It is hard to imagine why this is not the case for everyone selling property. However, it would be wrong to assume that everyone is like you. There are people who, for whatever reason, need to get their hands on money fast.

One of the disadvantages of property is that it is not a liquid asset. If you want to turn your asset into cash, generally it takes two to three months to complete a sale on a property, and that is once you've found a willing buyer. Even if you do find a buyer, there is no guarantee that the sale will go through; according to the Department of Trade and Industry, approximately one in three sales falls through in the UK.

Unfortunately, some people cannot afford to wait for two to three months to get the money from their property. They need the money now or at least within a few weeks. For these motivated sellers, the speed and reliability of the sale is more important than the actual amount of cash they generate from the sale. If you're able to help these people to get the cash they need in the time that they need it, they may be prepared to sell you their property for less than it's worth. You need to put yourself in their shoes to try and understand the situation the seller may be in.

So let's consider some of the reasons why sellers could be motivated to sell below the true market value:

Repossession:

Many people in the UK are in debt. As well as their mortgages, they have personal loans, credit cards, and they simply cannot keep up with all the payments. The danger is that if they don't keep up their payments, their property may get repossessed and they will lose their home. If your property is repossessed you get kicked out of your home. There is the public humiliation and embarrassment, your credit rating is ruined and it is very difficult to get funding in the future. If the house is sold for less than it's worth, you probably won't get any of the equity from the sale. In fact, if the sale of the property doesn't generate enough money to cover your mortgage balance and all the costs, you may be pursued by the mortgage company for up to 12 years after the repossession.

Unfortunately, repossessions are on the increase in the UK. Due to the Credit Crunch in America and the impact this has had on UK lenders, many people are finding it very difficult to refinance their existing mortgages and, as a result, they are falling into arrears if they cannot afford to keep up the payments.

More and more people who find themselves in this position would prefer to sell their property below market value rather than having it repossessed. Although the seller will not get the full market value from their property, at least they get to clear their debts, their credit record remains intact, and they have some chance of starting again.

Cash flow problems:

Occasionally you hear of perfectly good, successful and profitable companies that go out of business due to cash flow issues. Imagine the scenario where a successful business owner has, over the years, wisely reinvested the profit from their business back into residential property. However, in tough economic times maybe that business is now struggling and the business owner decides that they need to inject some cash into the business to save it. Selling some of their investment properties BMV to raise some cash quickly to support the business would be preferable to their business going bust!

Many amateur investors believe that motivated sellers are only people at the bottom end of the market. This is incorrect.

Wealthy people can also have cash flow issues which could be solved by selling some of their assets such as investment properties.

Downsizing:

This often occurs as people get older. Imagine a married couple who have been living in their good-sized home with their kids for a number of years. But maybe the kids have left home now and the two adults are rattling around in a large house. They decide to move to a smaller home or relocate to a warmer climate overseas where property may well be cheaper. If you were retiring and found your dream cottage or bungalow to retire to, you might decide that in order to secure your dream bungalow, you had to sell your house very quickly and so selling at a discount could be preferable to losing out on your dream home.

Emigrating:

When people move overseas, they sometimes decide that they want to dispose of property in the UK because they don't want the hassle of looking after it or maintaining it when they are away. In addition to this, people may need to sell their UK property to build or purchase overseas. In this instance, sellers will often accept a price below the true market value if it means they can move quickly and fulfill their dreams overseas.

Broken chain:

With approximately one in three house sales in the UK falling through, it is no wonder that selling a property can be a very frustrating and upsetting business. Imagine if you are trying to sell your property and your buyer had pulled out, not just once but twice. You may be pretty motivated to sell your property, because otherwise you may feel you'll never get to sell and move on. Anyone who has owned a property for a long time will have experienced some fantastic capital growth in their property, and may not need all the equity in the property in order to move on to the next property, especially if they are downsizing. Potentially, selling the property quickly for less than it is worth may be a good solution to allow them to move on and get on with their life.

Deceased estate:

Often when people inherit property, they don't know what to do with it. It may be located on the other side of the country. It may need work or maintenance and it may be inherited by several different people. The beneficiaries may decide that selling the property is better than holding on to it, so they can all get cash from the sale. Depending on personal circumstances, some of the beneficiaries may need money sooner than others, and so may be happy to sell the property for less than it is worth.

Divorce:

Unfortunately, 40% of marriages end in divorce these days. Sometimes, things get a bit messy and the two partners just want to split as quickly as possible and get on with their lives. The sale of the family home can often take a long time and cause unnecessary heartache. In this circumstance, the sellers may be prepared to sell the property for less than it is worth just so they can split the assets and get on with their separate lives.

Undesirable Property:

Sometimes property just does not seem to sell because it does not look very nice, needs too much doing to it, or could even be one of those 'Smelly Houses' – you know what I mean!

Maybe the property needs too much work doing to it so that it may not be eligible for a mortgage in its current condition. This would put off the majority of investors and so the property may remain on the market until it is offered at a price low enough to make the project viable.

The common theme

You may have noticed with all of the above reasons for being a motivated seller that there is a common theme. In all of the situations described, the seller had a property-related problem.

As a property entrepreneur, you are a property problem-solver. Solve someone's problem and you will get rewarded financially. It is your job to find out exactly what the problem is and work out a solution to the problem that works for you and the seller.

How to find motivated sellers

Most people who are selling property will want to achieve the highest possible price. Maybe only about every three or four people out of every 100 people selling their property will be motivated enough to give you the kind of discount you want. As a property problem solver, you have to become good at finding motivated sellers. The good news for you is there are motivated sellers absolutely everywhere. All you have to do is find them.

There are many shrewd investors in the UK who realise that buying property below market value from motivated sellers is probably the best investing strategy, no matter what the current market conditions. This means there is competition in the market. You need to make sure you stand out from the competition. There are two ways of doing this. Firstly, you need to make sure your marketing message is strong to get sellers to call you; secondly you need to make sure that the seller is persuaded to deal with you, rather than any other investor.

There are a number of different ways of finding motivated sellers. In this section we will briefly consider a number of strategies. To bring these strategies to life, I have asked some of the investors on my Property Mastermind Programme if they would provide some case studies of actual deals they have done. With their permission, some of the details of these deals are outlined below for your benefit.

Estate Agents

Not surprisingly, my very first property purchase was from an estate agent. So were the next seven properties I purchased before I worked out how to get motivated sellers to come direct to me. If you want to buy a property, it makes sense to go and speak to someone who represents lots of sellers. You would think that estate agents would be an excellent source of motivated sellers. After all, the estate agents will know when a sale has fallen through, or if the seller needs to sell in a particular hurry.

This is all good in theory, but I often hear investors complain that they cannot get any good deals from estate agents, because the estate agent has a shortlist of investors who they call first, whenever they get a really good deal. Generally, this is true and so many investors don't bother to look for motivated sellers at estate agents, because they think the agents will give all the best deals to their friends.

Estate agents aren't stupid. If they have a good deal that they can sell by calling one person rather than having to show 10 people around the property, what do you think they would rather do? I can tell you right now, some of the best deals I have had came from estate agents. I have sometimes been told about properties that are for sale before the "For Sale" board goes up, and even before the agent has produced the sale particulars for the property. If one of the local agents, with whom I work, finds a property that suits my criteria, they will always call me first, because they know if it is right, I will buy it. It saves them a lot of time and hassle, and it gives the seller a fast and certain solution to their problem.

As an investor, one of your goals should be to get on your local Estate Agent's shortlist, so that you are one of the people they call, whenever they get a good deal. The mistake that most amateur investors make is; that they walk into an estate agent and ask the estate agent for all their motivated sellers, explaining that they want to buy property 20% or more below market value.

In response to this, most estate agents will usually roll their eyes and think 'Here is another one, I have heard this all before! Another know it all, time wasting investor!' As soon as the amateur investor leaves the office, their business card will be promptly put in the rubbish bin and the estate agent will never think of them again. It is no surprise that most investors struggle to get great deals from estate agents.

You need to understand how to speak to estate agents in such a way that they want to do business with you.

You need to demonstrate to the estate agent that:

- **You know what you're doing without sounding arrogant,** so that they feel you are asking them to help you because you see them as the expert. Even if you do know more than the Estate Agent, never let them know that.

- **You are a serious investor,** unlike all the other time wasting amateur investors.

- **You have money ready to invest** so that you can move as quickly as you say you can.

- **You act promptly, efficiently and professionally** which means you are not going to mess them or the sellers around.

It can take a while to build a trusting relationship with estate agents, but if you put the effort work in you should get good

results. You need to keep in touch with them on a regula
so that they remember you.

Instead of asking the estate agents directly, if they have any
motivated sellers, which may not get the response from the
agent that you want, there are five specific questions you can
use to identify the circumstances, which might mean that the
sellers' are motivated.

Here are the 5 questions to ask estate agents:

1. Do you have any empty properties?

There are four main reasons why a property could be empty:
If the property looks a bit trashed it could be a repossessed
property as often they are damaged on the way out by the
previous owner who understandably could be bitter about the
repossession; If it looks dated and in need of modernisation
(often with some furniture left in it); it could be a deceased
estate, as probably someone has lived there for a number of
years and not made any improvements to the property; If it is
in good condition, but empty with no furniture, then it could
well be that the seller has already moved to a new property
whilst trying to sell this one; and finally, if it looks a bit tired
and is being sold with some furniture in it, then it may well be
a former rental property that a landlord is selling. In all four
cases, as the property is sitting there empty, the seller could be
motivated to sell at a good price.

2. Do you have any property that has been on the market a long time?

This question will identify properties that are just not selling.
Maybe the price is too high or something about the property is
putting off potential buyers. It may well be that a sale had been
agreed and has fallen through on the property, which might
make the seller even more frustrated.

there is some scope for a discounted offer. ges in property prices by using website like com

3. Do you have any properties, where there is more than one agent selling it?

Often sellers will list their property with two agents or more in an attempt to find a buyer quickly. They may not be willing to sell at the price you are prepared to pay, but it is certainly worth a look. The agent may be worried that they will not earn any commission, if the other agent finds a buyer and so they may be more motivated to work with you, to find a win/win for the vendor and you.

4. Do you have any properties that are listed for sale or for rent?

You often find that people are keen to sell their property, but will consider renting for a while if they are unable to sell. This is perfect for you if you are looking for Purchase Lease Options, where by, you rent the property out with the right to buy in the future. We would normally pay the Estate Agent their fee, at the time we sign the contracts, otherwise they will not get paid until the end of the option period, which could be several years, so this may not be very popular with some agents. Remember, the agents need to see what is in it for them and the seller, if you want them to agree to anything slightly different from the norm.

5. Do you have any sellers who keep calling the office to see if there is any news on their sale?

This is a sure sign that the seller is getting desperate; every few days they call the estate agent to see if there is any news. Often the seller will not tell the agent the full details of their situation, but this behavior is a sure sign that they are desperate to sell and so there may be a deal there. This person may be starting to annoy the staff in the agency and, so when you ask this particular question, often a particular seller will spring to mind!

Once an agent gives you a lead you need to act quickly. First of all you need to find, from the Estate Agent, as much information as possible about the property, the seller and their circumstances. Very often the agent may not have the information that we would normally get from the seller and, so we need to arrange a visit to the property when the seller is there if at all possible.

That means usually asking for a viewing in the evening or at the weekend, outside of the normal estate agency working hours. We are not attempting to cut the agent out in any way, but it is always best, if we can speak seller direct, to truly find out what is important to them. Remember, if the seller is truly motivated, it is not always the most money they go for, but the need for speed and certainty. If you do meet the seller in person, ask then for their contact details in case you have any further questions.

Always give feedback to the Estate Agent to tell them about the viewing and share your thoughts. If you have made an offer to the seller, always pass it through the agent as well, to make sure they don't think you are trying to cut them out of the deal. If the offer is not accepted, tell them that you will leave it on the table and make sure you follow up every few weeks, to see if they have become more motivated so that they will now consider your offer.

Once you have successfully completed a purchase through an Estate Agent, you need to go straight back to them and tell them that you are looking for another purchase. As you have just demonstrated that you are a serious investor, they will take you far more seriously than other investors interested in the same kind of deals. You will have worked your way onto their shortlist of preferred investors they call, whenever they get a good deal.

CASE STUDY: Nicki and Pete Uglow

When we first joined the Mastermind Programme we were asked to set an objective of what we wanted to achieve in the 12-month period. One of our first objectives was to earn enough passive income for me to be able to give up my full-time job. So we decided to set a strategy of buying student lets in Coventry as we know the local market, having both studied at Coventry University, and we knew that student properties would give us the great cash flow we wanted.

The main strategy we used to find motivated sellers was through estate agents. This is one of the first strategies we were taught and it seemed to work incredibly well for us. At the time, we were regularly buying properties at 18% to 23% below market value. Our very best deal came from a property that I found with an estate agent that was listed on the Rightmove website. It was a large house split into five flats. The value of this should have been about £500,000; I couldn't believe it when I saw it listed for sale at £166,000. That was 66% BMV. I thought there had to be some sort of mistake, but still I contacted the estate agent and, to my surprise, I found that he didn't seem very enthusiastic about this.

He said that lots of investors had been interested at that price but there was a problem and so no-one had been able to buy it. We know that whenever something is sold by a motivated seller there's a problem and we were taught to look for the solution rather than focus on the problem. What had happened was an investor had purchased this house and then converted it into five individual flats to increase the value. Unfortunately, he had forgotten to apply for planning permission. The local council somehow found out about it and slapped a restriction on the property such that it had to be converted back into a family home.

The investor ran out of money, could not afford to do anything with the property and eventually it was repossessed. The bank inherited the problem of a half-converted property that had a planning restriction on it. Anyone who purchased the property would have to turn it back into a family home which frankly wouldn't be worth £500,000 in this particular area. If you had that kind of money you would probably live somewhere else.

Not to be put off by this, I spoke to the planning department to find out exactly what was the problem. It turned out that the council didn't like the idea of having more flats in this particular area. Thinking creatively, I suggested to the planning officer that it was a real shame that we weren't able to use this property because my husband, being an ex-policeman, was thinking about letting the property to some policemen as we thought this would help the local area. This helped open up the conversation, after which we found a way of keeping the council happy and getting what we wanted; a true win/win.

Once the planning issue was resolved, we purchased the property at 66% off the true market value, using someone else's money for the deposit. We spent some money on finishing the refurbishment, and then were able to re-mortgage six months later, take out all of the money and some extra tax-free cash. The property has none of our money invested and produces a passive income after all costs of about £1,000 per month.

A summary of the deal is as follows:

- Value of the property was £499,000 which we agreed to purchase for £166,000 – a 66% discount.

- We put in a deposit of £44,000 using someone else's money.

- We spent about £85,000 completing the half-finished refurbishment

- After six months we re-mortgaged to £262,500, which gave us back all of our initial investment and just over £10,000 tax-free cash out.

- The property is rented out and brings in a gross rent of £26,520 per annum.

- After all monthly expenses we make just over £1,000 per month positive cash flow.

During our 12 months on the Property Mastermind Programme we purchased 10 student properties in Coventry worth approx £1.8m, using other people's money. We now enjoy a passive income after all expenses of approx £60,000 per year from these properties. This has changed our lives and we now have enough property so that we can pursue other interests.

Newspaper adverts

If you pick up a copy of your local free newspaper and look in the property section, you will always find adverts from buyers who are offering to purchase property for cash with fast completion. Depending on where you live, there may be lots of buyers advertising in this way. The reason they are advertising there is because it works. If it didn't work, they wouldn't be advertising, week in, week out. Some of the buyers advertising are national companies but many of them will be local investors just like you and me.

The investors I work with often feel it is not worth advertising in newspapers because of all the competition. I will acknowledge that yes, there may be lots of buyers advertising in your local newspaper, but I would put money on the fact that at least half of them don't really know what they're doing. A lot of people will see someone else using a certain strategy and try to copy it, without really understanding it. I have called many buyers advertising in newspapers, just to check out the competition. I was shocked at how amateurish most of the people are who answer the phone and how bad they are at asking the right questions. So yes, there are other investors advertising but I don't see them as competition, nor should you as long as you know what you're doing.

You will need to run your newspaper adverts over several months. Don't expect to place the advert just once and get an amazing response. If you get a call from a motivated seller who has seen your advert in the newspaper, there is a good chance they would have called some of the other advertisers as well. You need to be really good at building rapport on the telephone and move very quickly to take advantage of the deal, otherwise your competition will beat you to it.

Copy writing guidelines

People have written entire books about copy writing, but I want to give you a really quick lesson in how to get a better response from your adverts.

There are three key components to any advert. They are: The Headline, The Body Copy and The Call to Action.

The Headline: This has to grab the attention of the reader, make them stop and want to read more about your product or service. Decide what type of seller you are aiming to attract.

The Body Copy: This is where you promote the benefits of your service. This should explain what's in it for the reader! You need to target your message to appeal to the reader.

The Call to Action: This is where you tell the reader what you want them to do next. Call you now on a certain number. What do you want them to do if they are interested in your service?

Case Study: Dean and Mandy Purkiss

Dean and I started to invest in 2004 and in five years we managed to purchase 8 investment properties, then we ran out of deposit money. We then heard about the Property Mastermind Programme and realised that we did not have to use our money, to build our cash flow generating property portfolio.

We Joined the Property Mastermind Programme in April 2010 and out of all the lead generation strategies we were taught, we found that newspaper advertising was by far the best response in our area.

One day we received a message from our call answering service to say, that Mrs X had phoned and seemed somewhat annoyed that we had not called her back. This was initially confusing because we ensure we always call people back when we say we will, and also we did not recognise her name or address!

Dean telephoned Mrs X and discovered she had in fact spoken to another investor, who advertises in the same newspaper, who had not bothered to call her back! Dean then asked about her situation and discovered that her reason for selling was due to her ill health, and her desire to move into a smaller property, because she had lost her husband.

Dean thought we could probably help her and arranged for me to visit the property and sit down with Mrs X to find a win/ win solution.

Prior to visiting the property, I did my research and found the property was already being advertised by an estate agent at a significantly reduced price of £115k. Similar properties on the same street were being marketed at £160k -£170k. I also checked the previous sold prices in the area and this confirmed to me that the property was greatly reduced.

When I met with Mrs X at the property, she explained that she had already found somewhere much smaller, that she wanted to move to, but needed to sell her property first. She said that she wanted to be able to sell quickly to move on and have some 'pension' money in her bank account. She was struggling to stay on top of the cleaning in the house and found, due to her health, that it was extremely difficult climbing the stairs. She had contacted another investor in the paper who was supposed to get back to her, but after a week she had not heard from them. I assured her that would definitely not happen with us and so she was happy to move forward with the deal as agreed.

I noticed several positive things while I was viewing the property. It had three double bedrooms and a separate downstairs dining room so it was perfect for a multi-let. The location was ideal, as it is extremely convenient to the town centre and the property required no work.

After building a rapport with Mrs X and finding out what she needed, we agreed on a purchase price of £85,000. This enabled Mrs X to move on to a property much better suited to her needs. The sale progressed within 6 weeks and during that time, we kept Mrs X updated with regard to the situation and everything progressed smoothly.

Summary of this deal is as follows:

- True market value of the property £160,000 with an agreed purchase price of £85,000 (47% BMV).

- We obtained a 75% BTL mortgage and used other people's money for the deposit.

- Six month's later the property was re-mortgaged to remove all of the deposit and so there is now no money left in the property.

- Let out as a multi-let property this makes £650 positive cash flow each month after all bills and expenses.

- There is £75,000 equity left in the property.

This is just one of the 16 extra properties we have purchased since April 2010; we have also sourced and sold a further 25 properties for other investors, which has made us over £80,000. We also now have a passive rental income of £7500 per month. This means we have now both been able to give up full time work, and spend far more quality time with our kids. We love working in our property business and helping people solve their property problems.

Postcards

This is an incredibly easy, cost-effective method of finding motivated sellers. However, many people overlook this method because it almost seems too simple. Investors don't believe that it would work, but it does. The basic idea is you create a small advert which you can place in the window of local corner shops or newsagents for a minimal cost each week. The copy on the postcard adverts would be very similar to that of a newspaper advert or leaflet. It just happens to be the same advert on show in one location for months and months on end. This method may not generate a lot of leads for you, but it does work as long as you have enough postcards in different shops. Don't be surprised if you don't get any response from the two postcards you have displayed, as that is not enough. Ideally you want hundreds of postcards all over the areas in which you invest.

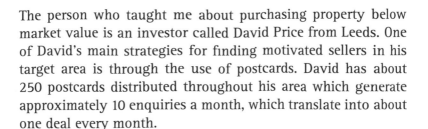

The person who taught me about purchasing property below market value is an investor called David Price from Leeds. One of David's main strategies for finding motivated sellers in his target area is through the use of postcards. David has about 250 postcards distributed throughout his area which generate approximately 10 enquiries a month, which translate into about one deal every month.

Leafleting

The idea behind this strategy is that you can target specific areas in which you would like to buy below market value properties. In essence, you design a leaflet which explains the service and have this delivered to 15,000 to 20,000 households in your target area. To achieve good results, you do need to deliver high numbers of leaflets, but the benefit of this strategy is that you are going direct to the seller and thus may have less competition than if they were to respond to an advert in a newspaper.

This strategy requires some capital input to pay for printing and distribution of your leaflets plus it does take some time and effort to coordinate. But the results can be well worth the time and effort required.

It is not a good use of your time to distribute these leaflets yourself. You can either pay Royal Mail to do it for you or recruit your own team of leaflet distributors. Running your own team does take some effort and you need to put checks in place to ensure people are doing what they are supposed to do.

I do not recommend you put your leaflets in with the local free newspaper; the response rate will fall dramatically as most people put these leaflets straight in the bin.

Websites

One of the quickest and easiest ways to attract motivated sellers is through the internet. However, on the internet you will face a lot of competition from other property problem solvers. If a motivated seller completes an application form on your website, you can bet that they have filled in applications on a number of other websites as well. Often it is the first property problem solver to contact the seller who will secure the deal, as long as that investor knows what they are doing. Speed, as always, is critical here.

Buying leads from other investors

If you don't want to set up your own lead-generating systems, you may decide that the easier route for you to find motivated sellers is buying leads from other investors. I have found some fantastic investment opportunities, which have come from other investors, like the one I described earlier for which I paid the investor a finder's fee.

CASE STUDY: Tony Law

I'm a property investor based in Bournemouth and over the years, I have bought and sold my fair share of properties. My strategy has always been to buy, refurbish and sell on - hopefully at a profit, although I would have to hold my hand up and say this hasn't always been the case.

Early in 2010 I read Simon's book "Property Magic" and, although the book was laid out well and gave clear guidance on the techniques necessary to become successful in property, I would have to say there was one element in it that I really struggled with. It was the idea, that it was possible to genuinely buy property at below market value. After all - why would anyone (in their right minds) sell their property at anything other than the full market value? It just didn't make any sense!

Some months later, I heard there was a property investing event being held at the Excel centre in London and, I knew

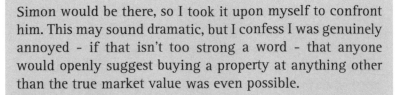

Simon would be there, so I took it upon myself to confront him. This may sound dramatic, but I confess I was genuinely annoyed - if that isn't too strong a word - that anyone would openly suggest buying a property at anything other than the true market value was even possible.

Anyway, after spending a bit of time wandering around, talking to the other exhibitors, I had the opportunity to approach Simon on his stand and I asked my question. "Simon", I said, "I have been in property for a number of years. I understand you can get a better deal by seeking out motivated sellers, however, I don't believe it is actually possible to buy a property at anything like 25% below market value, in my neck of the woods". I will never forget Simon's answer. It was certainly not the answer I was expecting and it completely threw me. He asked me where I lived and then replied: "That explains it! You are absolutely right; Bournemouth is the only area in the UK where there has never been a repossession!"

This unexpected answer made me realize that maybe I had not looked at it from the motivated seller's point of view.

Following our conversation, I decided that I probably needed to open my mind up to the possibility that, maybe under certain circumstances, some people would sell their property for less than it is worth.

I decided to invest in my education and signed up for my wife and myself to attend Simon's one-day Property Investing Quick Start seminar.

One day with Simon, answered many of my questions and within a month, I had found my first true motivated seller lead in my area, which I purchased from another investor, over the internet for just £49.

The property in question was a three bedroom semi detached house in Parkstone, Poole. Although externally the house was fine, to be honest, internally this house was pretty awful. There was dirt, junk and even animal "deposits" everywhere, although I have to say the owners themselves were lovely people. They had a strong desire to move back to South Wales and since the husband was disabled, houses that might be suitable for the husbands needs, did not come up very often. Since their own house was obviously going to prove difficult to sell and since suitable houses to buy in Wales, came up pretty infrequently, they decided to sell their house at a discount, to put them in a much stronger position to buy when the right house did came up - just so long as I was willing to accept a delayed completion - which I was happy to do.

As it happens, their ideal house turned up shortly after we agreed the deal and so the transaction was carried through conventionally.

Despite some very convincing comparables ranging from between £155,000 to £175,000, I managed to negotiate a purchase price of £110,000. This property did need a bit of work however, which cost me a further £16,000, so all in all, my BMV deal, with costs, came out at £126,000. Four months later the property was re-valued at £165,000, which I still feel is too cheap, but since this house is now bringing in £895.00 per month, I have no intention of selling it anyway.

Summary of this deal as follows:

- I purchased this motivated seller lead for £49 from another investor.

- Property worth £165,000 purchased for £110,000.

- £16,000 of renovation required so true purchase price is £126,000.

- Re-mortgaged to £123,750 (75% LTV) so less than £3k left in the property with over £40k equity in the property.

- Rental income is £895 per month which after all the expenses, leaves me with a positive cash flow of £250 per month.

So, do I now believe it is possible to buy BMV in Bournemouth - you better believe it! And that was the problem before, because I did not believe it, I was looking for evidence to prove myself right. Now that I know that it can be done I am actively looking for more deals.

There are two main ways of finding leads from other investors:

The internet: There are several websites which specialise in attracting motivated sellers, and then sell the leads on to other property problem solvers. This can be a very quick and easy way to find deals. However, you need to be prepared to work through a number of leads which may not be suitable until you find a good deal. You also have to be quick as there may be many other investors using this route to find leads.

Networking: This is by far the best way to find leads from other investors, by getting to know other investors and building trusting working relationships. You can get to the position where other people are finding deals and bringing them to you for a finder's fee. The benefit of this over the internet is that you may have exclusivity on deals offered to you. In my Property Mastermind group, we have an online forum where Mastermind members can share deals with each other. There is a high level of trust within my Property Mastermind group so that people work ethically together.

You must be ethical

When some people hear about the way we buy property below market value, they question the ethics behind our motives. Some people may think that we're taking advantage of people in a vulnerable position. This is not the case. I'm sure there are investors out there who do take advantage of motivated sellers but this is not my style. I believe that if I approach the deal ethically, if I am open and honest with the seller and find a true WIN/WIN deal that could help them and me, I am offering a service and providing a solution to their problem.

I'm about to give you probably the most valuable piece of information with regard to buying properties below market value. Are you ready for this? The most important piece of advice I would give any investor who is looking to buy property BMV from a motivated seller is this:

Whenever you meet a motivated seller, always hold their best interests in your heart. You should constantly ask yourself the question, "How can I help this person?" If you come at this from the direction of trying to help people, you will stand head and shoulders above the rest of the competition. Before I buy a property from anybody, I make sure that selling their property to me really is their best option. This is so important that I want to spend a whole chapter focusing on ethics and dealing with motivated sellers.

Chapter 4:

You should buy property ethically for a WIN/WIN solution

Dealing with motivated sellers

I am constantly amazed at the number of investors I meet who appeared to stumble across motivated sellers, but who have no idea how to deal with the vendor. If you want the motivated seller to work with you, rather than another investor, you need to make sure that they are confident that you can deliver on your promise. You need to ensure that you provide a prompt, professional and courteous service from the very initial contact right up to completion.

The first thing you need to consider is the initial point of contact. So let's say you have an advert in the local newspaper, have built your relationship with estate agents and/or carried out your first leaflet campaign. What happens when your first motivated seller calls you? Do you know what to say to them? Do you know what information you need to gain from them? Do you know how to build rapport with them? If you don't make the right first impression, or even worse you expect them to leave their details on your answer-phone, they will just call the next person advertising in the newspaper.

You have to be there, ready to take their call. If you can't be there because maybe you still work full-time, delegate this to someone else. Do you know someone who could answer the phone for you? If not, maybe you should use one of those 24-hour answering services who will take the caller's details at any time of the day and send you a message by email, text or whatever is the most convenient format for you.

Whenever a motivated seller contacts you, you need to be quick. Remember, the whole motivation is around speed so time is very valuable to them. There are certain key pieces of information which you need to acquire from the motivated seller to assess if this is a suitable deal for you or not.

Details you need to get from the seller:

- Their name and contact details, preferably landline and

mobile telephone numbers.

- The full address and postcode of the property they want to sell.

- Is it freehold or leasehold? If leasehold, how long is left on the lease and what are the service charges?

- A full description of the property, including:

  > Style of property e.g. terraced, semi, detached, bungalow or flat.

  > Number of bedrooms, bathrooms and living rooms.

  > Does it have double glazing, central heating, extensions or garage?

  > Have they done any work to the property such as new kitchen, wiring etc?

- The reason they are selling the property.

- Their estimated valuation of the property and reasons to justify their estimate.

- The amount of the mortgage plus any arrears or redemption penalties.

- Are there any other investors interested?

- The particular timescales to which they are working.

- When would be a good time to come and view the property?

These basic details will enable you to do your initial research to assess if there is a deal or not. Armed with this information, a few selected websites and a telephone, within about 20 minutes you can assess the opportunity to see if it is right for you.

You need to build rapport with the seller to get them to give you this information. It's no good rushing in, asking them how much they need and telling them you will only pay less than it is worth, until you have a chance to explain what you do and put them at ease that they're dealing with a professional. You need to reassure the seller that your conversation is in complete confidence. You need to understand the seller's situation and try to put yourself in their shoes and understand how they will be feeling. They need a solution to their problem, and they need it quickly. That is why they are prepared to sell their house for less than it is worth.

Many investors feel that they can win a deal by outbidding the competition. This is not always the case. A few years ago, I went to visit a motivated seller in Derby. We'll call her Sarah. Sarah and her husband wanted to sell their house so they could move on to a new property. The property was listed with an estate agent, and they had already had one sale fall through. They had no confidence in the estate agent and decided to try and sell the property privately, which is why they contacted me. While I was at the property building rapport with Sarah, I found out that she had also contacted two other companies. The first company she spoke to was very impersonal on the phone and she didn't like them. The second company had been to visit her and had made her an offer. Based on my research, I estimated the property was worth about £160,000. I calculated that I could offer Sarah £130,000 for the property. I had built a really good rapport with Sarah, and she told me that the other company had actually offered her more money, but she said that if I could match the offer, she would sell the property to me. I said I would go back to the office and look at my numbers again to see if I could increase my offer. I liked Sarah and I really wanted to help her. I thought about increasing my offer to £132,000 but it just wouldn't work for me. So I phoned Sarah about an hour later and explained that I was really sorry, but based on my figures, I could only offer her £130,000. I said that I was sorry I couldn't help and I recommended she should take the higher offer, which I believe was about £134,000. Sarah said that was a real shame, and she really wanted to deal with me because she trusted me. Thirty minutes later, I had a phone call from Sarah, who said she had just spoken to her husband and they had agreed to accept my offer and sell to me for £130,000. So the person who offers the most money doesn't always get the property; it is all about the relationship you develop with the seller.

Is everybody ethical?

There was a lot of negative media coverage in the press towards the end of 2007 regarding investors who were apparently ripping off desperate sellers, particularly when it came to Sale and Rent Back which is why the FSA introduced the SARB requirements in July 2009.

Due to this negative press, some sellers (and their friends and family) can sometimes be sceptical of your motives. I am very upfront with sellers to whom I speak. I explain that I am not a charity and that I want to make money from any deal that we agree but it is also important for me to make sure that we find a WIN/WIN solution to their problem so that they are happy.

Everyone is better off with a WIN/WIN deal

When you start advertising for motivated sellers you will no doubt speak to some people who are desperate to sell their property. However, there is absolutely no need to take advantage of these sellers. After all, you want to sleep at night with a clear conscience. I believe that if you find a WIN/WIN deal, you are genuinely helping the seller and providing a solution to their problem.

Remember the question at the end of the last chapter, "How can I help this person solve their problem?" The best way to do this is to ask the seller what they want. Find out what is really important to them and see if you can give them what they need. When I agree to buy property, the price I agree is the amount the seller will actually receive. There are no hidden fees or charges and I will offer to cover the cost of their solicitor. If the seller is in debt, I only want to buy the property if I can help them to clear all of their debts with the proceeds from the sale of their property. I always find out how much they owe in total. Sometimes they are in so much debt that I just can't help them, in which case I might refer them to a reputable debt management company who may be able to help them.

Don't mess people around

It can be extremely stressful for a vendor trying to find someone to buy their property. If the individual needs to sell by a certain time it can be even worse. It is really important that you as a potential buyer don't give the vendor false hope. Don't tell someone you can purchase their property if you have no intention of doing so. These people don't have a lot of time and so you cannot afford to waste it. You need to be quick and decisive. If you can't help them, tell them so they can move on and find another buyer. If you can help them, make sure you stick to your word. You need to give the seller certainty that you will do what you say you will do, when you say will do it. I recommend you keep a diary and use it to schedule the time when you need to call the seller to keep them updated on progress of the sale of their property.

Communication is really important. Keep in touch with the seller throughout the process to let them know what is happening at every stage of the transaction. Remember the selling and buying process is probably a lot more stressful for the seller than it is for you. I learnt this the hard way.

When I first started to buy property this way, I lost a deal because I did not keep the seller updated as to what was happening. I agreed the purchase on a property in Birmingham on the Tuesday morning and said I would call the seller 'later'. What I meant by this was that I would call when I had some news. The seller thought I meant later that day! In her mind, when I did not call when I said I would, she thought I had lost interest and so called another investor.

I had not wanted to call her until I had some positive news on the progress of the sale. So when I finally called on the Thursday morning with the news that the surveyor would be coming round the following day, she was rather surprised to hear from me and said that she had agreed a deal with someone else.

My poor communication had just caused me to lose a deal worth £25,000 in equity. Don't make the same costly mistake as I did. Find out the expectations of the seller in terms of how often they want to hear from you, and make sure you keep the rapport going.

The Motivated Seller code of ethics

Along with several members of my Property Mastermind Programme, we have created a code of ethics and I insist that everybody on my Programme follows it. Many of my investors actually show this code of ethics to potential sellers to reassure them that they are going to serve the seller as best they can:

- Any information disclosed to me by the seller will be treated with the utmost confidence.

- We commit to finding the best WIN/WIN deal for all the parties concerned.

- If we believe that selling your property to us is not the

best solution for you, we will tell you and even help you with an alternative solution.

- We commit to providing realistic timescales for the purchase of their property.

- We guarantee that there are no hidden costs for the seller. The price we agree is the amount you will receive.

- We will keep you informed and updated throughout the purchase process.

- We will do what we say we will do and keep to our word.

If you come from a place of trying to help the seller find a WIN/WIN solution you will get more deals.

Chapter 5:

A new strategy for
property investors.

When revising this 4th edition of Property Magic, I wanted to take the opportunity to add this new chapter about how you can use and profit from property Options.

Purchase Options have been used for many years in the area of commercial property and development, for example in relation to land purchases, however the use of Purchase Lease Options in residential property investing is relatively new here in the UK, despite being established in the USA and Australia.

There is a great deal of ignorance and misunderstanding surrounding the topic of Property Options and whether or not they are legal. Please don't expect to learn everything you need to know about Options in just one chapter. I am currently writing a book about Options and it is going to be a big book. However, the purpose of this chapter is to give you an awareness of Purchase Options, and an understanding of what they are and, more importantly, you can use them for mutual benefit of you and the motivated seller.

What are Purchase Options and Purchase Lease Options?

A Purchase Option is a legal agreement, which gives you the control of an asset without actually owning it.

To keep it simple, I'm going to break it down into its various elements;

- An Option is the right to buy but not the obligation to do so,

- at a fixed price,

- within a certain time period.

Taking this one step further, a Purchase Lease Option is the same as a Purchase Option, with the additional benefit of being able to use the assets in return for a monthly payment (rental/ lease payment).

What this means is, that you can control a property and gain a rental income from it, without the need for the usual 25% deposit or even a mortgage!

This can be extremely attractive to anyone who wants to invest in property, but for whatever reason is unable to obtain a mortgage and or does not have a large deposit.

It sounds too good to be true!

Very often when investors first hear about Options, they are skeptical because the concept sounds too good to be true. Why on earth would the seller agree to grant you an option on their property?

Remember the underlying essence of this book is all about you finding motivated sellers who have a property related problem and, then creating an ethical win/win solution. In certain circumstances, a Purchase Lease Option could be the ideal solution for the seller.

The easiest way to explain this is with an example:

Peter is the owner of a property, which in today's market is worth about £100,000, and he has a mortgage on the property of £98,000. In this situation, there would be absolutely no point in you making Peter a below market value offer for his property, because he needs the full asking price to be able to clear the outstanding mortgage.

Even if Peter found a buyer who was prepared to purchase the property at the full market value, by the time he has paid estate agency and legal fees, it is unlikely that he will make any money from the sale of the property. This raises an interesting question. If Peter is not going to get any money from the sale, why is he selling?

It's really important to understand this point. Sometimes the vendor may be selling a property, not because they want to raise money from the sale, but simply because they do not want the property, or the mortgage debt associated with it.

Maybe the monthly payments on the mortgage are a financial burden to Peter that he would rather not have. Although the sale of the property would not raise any income, it would mean that he would no longer need to find the money to pay the mortgage each month. This could be a logical reason for Peter wanting to get rid of the property.

In this situation, maybe we can help Peter as follows: We say to Peter, that we would be prepared to purchase the property at full market value (or maybe slightly more) in a few years time, and in the meantime we make all of the monthly mortgage payments for him. In a way, we are babysitting Peter's mortgage for him. This could be a great solution for Peter, but what could possibly be in it for us?

Let's say that Peter's mortgage payments are £300 per month and this property would rent out for £550 a month. As long as the property is in an area with strong rental demand, then you could potentially benefit from a couple of hundred pounds from a property that you don't own.

Now you may be thinking, "If the cash flow on this property is so good, why doesn't the owner just rent out the property themselves?

One possible answer to this very valid question is that usually the owner doesn't want the hassle or risk of being a landlord. Maybe they're worried about bad tenants or void periods when they would need to cover the costs themselves. Maybe they have been a landlord previously and experienced some of these problems, and now they are just fed up and want to get rid of the problem.

The main benefit to the owner for granting you a Purchase Lease Option is that you commit to pay their mortgage every month, whether or not the property is tenanted. This piece of mind and certainty may be more important to the owner than making a few hundred pounds per month.

How do you like the idea of benefiting from the cash flow and potential equity growth without the need to get a mortgage in your own name?

How to spot a potential Purchase Lease Option

There are 2 specific criteria to look at, which will help you identify potential Purchase Lease Option deals.

The first and most important criteria, is that the vendor does not need money from the sale of the property. Most people who are selling a property are doing so because they do actually require the money for something. If that's the case, then a Purchase Lease Option would probably not be suitable for them because with the Option they are not going to receive the money they need now.

If however, they are selling the property because they don't want it, and they don't need the cash from the sale (or as in the example above with Peter, there may be no cash left after clearing the mortgage), then a Purchase Lease Option could be a viable solution.

Right now there are many properties for sale on the open market that have no equity, or are in negative equity, whereby the mortgage debt is higher than the value of the property. This is why this particular strategy can work very well in the current market conditions.

The second criteria to look at, is what I call favorable mortgage conditions. By this, I mean the owner's mortgage is ideally:

On a relatively low interest-rate: Due to the record low Bank of England base rate, many people are fortunate to be paying very low interest rates on their mortgages. These rates are often lower than the interest rate you would pay when taking out a new mortgage; which means by babysitting the owner's mortgage, the monthly payments may be less than the payments you would make on your mortgage, if you owned the property. Basically this means there is more cash flow profit for you every month.

Interest only mortgage: If the owner's mortgage is interest only, then the monthly payments will be less than if they have a repayment mortgage. It's not necessarily a deal breaker if the seller has a repayment mortgage, but you will make less monthly cash flow.

Buy to Let mortgage: If the owner has a residential mortgage, and you intend to rent out the property, then really you should seek approval from the owner's mortgage company, referred to as "consent to let". If the Seller is a landlord, then they will probably have a Buy to Let mortgage in which case it automatically has consent to let, which makes the process far easier for all concerned.

If both of these criteria are in place, then there is a good chance that a Purchase Lease Option could work well. Given the choice, most vendors would prefer a clean sale rather than a Purchase Lease Option, so you need to be able to simply explain how an Option could benefit both you and them.

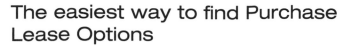

The easiest way to find Purchase Lease Options

By now you are probably thinking. "This sounds great. How do I find vendors who would be happy to grant me a Purchase Lease Option on their property?"

Instead of just looking for Purchase Lease Options which, remember, will not be a viable solution for many vendors; particularly those who are selling because they need the cash now. A more successful strategy maybe to focus on finding motivated sellers (as described earlier in this book), for which some of whom, Purchase Lease Options could be an appropriate solution.

Having said this, I want to highlight two particular types of motivated sellers for whom Purchase Lease Options could work really well.

The first type is the vendor who has a property listed with an Estate Agent and a letting agent at the same time. I am sure you will have noticed this in the past.

This would suggest that the vendor probably wants to sell, but is struggling to do so and thus is prepared to rent until they can sell. This is exactly what you are proposing with a Purchase Lease Option. You will pay them a monthly rent until you buy it at some point in the future.

The second type of vendor is the tired or retiring landlord, who no longer wants the hassle of their Buy to Let property. I find that this type of vendor may also be more open to creative solutions than the average motivated seller. You can find these landlords by looking in newspapers or online for landlords who are renting their properties out or you may even meet them at property networking events.

What to say to property owners?

When speaking to a vendor never use the words Purchase Lease Option, as most people will have no idea what you are talking about. You need to keep the language really simple, make sure you understand their problem and then demonstrate how you can solve their problem.

There are two simple questions you can ask the property owner to determine, if they would consider granting you a Purchase Lease Option on their property.

1. "Would you be interested in renting your property on a long term let for between 3 to 5 years?"

2. "Would you be interested in selling the property to me at some point in the future?"

If they answer yes to both of these questions, then there is a good chance that a Purchase Lease Option could work. It then comes down to a matter of negotiation around the purchase price, the length of the option and the monthly payment.

What about legal contracts?

To make the Option agreement legally binding you need to pay a financial consideration to the seller in return for the Option to buy. This option fee is usually just £1, but depending on the nature and size of deal could be several thousand pounds.

One of the main benefits for you doing an Option is that you have the right to buy, but not the obligation to do so. The vendor, on the other hand is contractually obliged to sell to you if you want to exercise your Option to buy.

This could cause some potential problems. Imagine that you help a motivated seller who is now desperate to get rid of their property, which has no equity, and so you take on the responsibility to pay their mortgage and have the right to buy in five years at the current market value of £100k. In five years time that property could increase in value to say £135k. Five years can be a long time and the vendor may decide that they don't really want to sell you the property worth £135k for just £100k.

Whilst Option contracts are legally binding, and at the time the vendor was all too happy to sign, I predict that in the very near future there could be "no win, no fee" solicitors delighted to help vendors get out of these agreements because they may seem "unfair" or even claiming that the vendors did not know what they were agreeing to.

For this reason it is very important that both you and the Vendor obtain independent legal advice to ensure that everyone understands exactly what they are committing to.

The challenge here is that because Purchase Lease Options are quite new; most solicitors don't understand what they are and so could even put their clients off doing it.

For this reason, we always use two firms of solicitors from our power team, who understand options and work well together.

One firm represents you and the other one represents the Vendor to ensure that they understand the implications.

All you need to do is to agree the "Heads of Terms" with the Vendor and then forward these to your solicitor who will draw up the legal contracts for you.

The "Heads of Terms" need to include:

1. Your full name and home address.

2. The Vendor's full name and home address.

3. The address of the property in question.

4. The agreed option fee (at least £1).

5. The amount for which you can purchase the property.

6. The length of the Option period.

7. Any monthly lease (if applicable.)

What else can you do with Options?

There is so much you can do with Options. In this chapter, I have just scratched the surface but I wanted to make you aware of how these powerful tools could help you and some of the motivated sellers that you will find.

I am currently writing another book called "No Mortgage Required" all about Purchase Lease Options and how you can profit from using them.

For the time being, let me just share a few ideas on how you could use purchase lease options:

Upgrade your own living accommodation

When you take out a Purchase Lease Option on a property, you don't have to rent it out to a tenant. You could decide to live there yourself. One of my Mastermind delegates did this on a large empty property in the village where he lives. He has moved into this large house which was almost twice the size of his own home, and managed to rent out his own home for about the same amount as he pays in monthly Options fees. The net effect is that he now lives in a house twice the size of his own home, at no extra cost.

If you are currently renting yourself, this could also be a great way for you to get your foot onto the property ladder.

Flip property using Options

Many investors like the idea of buying property at a discount, adding some value and then selling it on at a higher price. Rather than having to put in a deposit and get a mortgage to buy the property, why not just control it with an Option and flip it through an auction or add value and, then sell it on.

Control an overseas holiday home

You can also use Purchase Lease Options on holiday homes. There are plenty of overseas property owners who do not want their properties any more, but are unable to sell them.

The owners may be happy to receive a low rental all year round with no hassle, which could allow you to make a huge profit renting the property out week by week in peak season.

If you are going to do this, you need to do your research, just as you would with any investment, to make sure there is sufficient rental demand in the area, at the correct rental rate to make it worth you while.

Multi let - high cash flow strategy

This is a strategy that we have taught on the Property Mastermind Programme for the last few years and is now becoming very popular, with the increasing popularity of multi-let properties, as described in the next chapter.

The idea is that you find a large property, which the landlord is struggling to rent out on a single let basis. You offer to pay the landlord a guaranteed rent for 3 to 5 years on a commercial lease. As long as the property is in the right location, it may be possible to rent out the individual rooms, which will achieve a rent far higher than the single let rent. This means you can make between £400 to £1000 profit on a property that you don't own or even have a mortgage on. How cool is that?

If you would like to be one of the first investors to receive details of my new book when it is launched, register your interest here now: www.NoMortgageRequiredBook.co.uk

Chapter 6:

How to maximise cash
flow from your property.

One of the main benefits of investing in property is the significant capital gain you can make as your property rises in value over the long term. However, to benefit from the gain you need to make sure you can afford to hold the property in the meantime. Ideally you don't want to have to support your property portfolio. Quite the opposite in fact! Your portfolio should support you financially. The rent you receive from your tenants should more than cover all the costs of ownership such that each month there is surplus cash profit left over for you to enjoy.

Investors who lose money are often the ones who get it wrong because of cash flow. They can't afford to hold their property and so have to sell which, depending on the market conditions, means they themselves may become motivated sellers. The purpose of this chapter is to help you ensure you maximise the cash flow from your investment properties.

So let's go back to fundamentals for a moment. As a property investor, one of the critical skills you need to develop is the ability to assess a particular opportunity quickly to decide if it is a good investment and suitable for you or not.

What makes a good investment?

Now let's just remind ourselves of the first three of my Five Golden Rules of Investing:

1. Always buy from motivated sellers.

2. Buy in an area with strong rental demand.

3. Buy for cash flow.

Of course you want to pay as little as ethically possible for the property but the discount alone is not the only factor to consider. There is no point buying a property even with a great

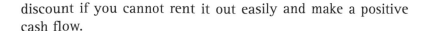

discount if you cannot rent it out easily and make a positive cash flow.

To help you focus on only buying good cash flow properties you could buy 'as if prices will never go up again' and so the only reason to buy would be for the great cash flow and return on investment.

When researching any potential investment there are two main factors we are concerned with. We want to determine:

A) The true market value of the property.

B) The realistic market rent that could be achieved.

This is the information that a mortgage company would want a Chartered Surveyor to collect, on their behalf, in order to assess whether to grant you a Buy to Let mortgage on a particular property. You need this information a long time before you even apply for the mortgage to decide if it is the right kind of investment for you.

With these two pieces of information you can ascertain whether you are going to make a profit each month after covering all of the expenses.

The main expense you will incur on a monthly basis is the interest on your Buy to Let mortgage. I have a very simple rule of thumb which you can use to assess this monthly expense.

For every £20,000 you borrow, at an interest rate of 6% you will pay £100 per calendar month (p.c.m) in interest. For example, if you were to borrow £80,000 it would cost you £400 p.c.m.

This is based on a 6% annual interest rate for two reasons: firstly it's the average rate I've had during my years of investing; secondly, it keeps the numbers easy to calculate because every £20,000 you borrow costs just £100 p.c.m. I like to keep things as simple as possible.

If the average cost of a mortgage is only 5% per annum then this rule of thumb is very conservative. This means that, in reality, £20,000 will not cost you as much as £100 p.c.m, but by using this in your calculations you are being very cautious, which is good because you don't want to be too optimistic.

When working out the cash flow, many investors are too optimistic on what the costs will be and they don't get it right. It's better to be pessimistic and have a nice surprise by making more money than expected.

Does the investment stack up?

The mortgage lender will then use a rent multiplier to make sure that the rent is going to be enough to cover the monthly interest and the other costs associated with the property.

This rent multiplier can vary from lender to lender but most will use something like 125%. This means that the lender wants to check that the monthly rent is 125% of the monthly interest payment (rent = monthly interest x 125%).

With a mortgage of £80,000 and a monthly interest charge of £400, your lender would generally want to see a monthly rental income of at least £500 (£400 x 125%).

The extra 25% over and above the interest payments is an approximation of the other monthly costs. Some of the other monthly costs involved in property are:

Buy To Let insurance: This is specialist landlord insurance which covers not only the building and the contents but also if someone was to have an accident in your property and they decide to sue you, your insurance would cover this as well.

Property management fees: You might have a letting agent looking after your property for you which will cost on average

10% of the rent each month. Many investors start by managing their own properties but I would suggest that, once you have a number of properties, you don't really want to do this. Using a letting agent will reduce your profit each month but you must value your own time. I doubt very much you want to just swap whatever your current job and replace it with a job as a full-time property manager. I recommend you find a good letting agent to manage your property for you to make sure you don't have the hassle.

Service charge: If it's a leasehold property you are going to have service charges which, calculated on a monthly basis, might be anywhere from £40 to £300 p.c.m depending on the facilities that are on offer at that particular development. The service charges pay for community facilities such as cleaning of the hallways, electricity in the hallways and maintenance of the building. The building might have a concierge or lifts that need maintaining which will increase the service charges. The costs can vary dramatically, so if you are buying a leasehold property it's really important to ask what the service charges are each month. There will also be a small ground rent charge which might be a few hundred pounds a year.

Central heating insurance: If you have a gas supply in your property then it is a legal requirement to have a Gas Safety Certificate which needs to be renewed each year. This can be done as part of your boiler insurance offered by British Gas and other suppliers. I have this insurance on all of my properties to make sure that if there's any problem with my central heating, I can get it fixed quickly at no cost to me. The other benefit is that the tenant calls the service supply direct, they don't call me. That's great because I don't get the hassle and they feel in control of resolving the issue. In my view, it's worth paying the insurance premium which is about £15 to £20 per month depending on the property.

Using the rent multiplier will help you to assess very quickly if a property is going to make monthly cash flow for you. With a monthly interest cost of £400, if the monthly rent was just £500, it may only just about cover the costs. However, if the monthly rent was £550, then it means you would probably make some cash flow from this property each month. If the rent was just £450, you wouldn't be making positive cash flow; in fact we know it's going to cost you around £50 each month. In reality the lender may not lend the full amount.

To summarise; you can work out quickly if a property stacks up as follows:

1. Work out how much the mortgage going to cost you.

2. Multiply the monthly interest by 125% to give the required rent.

3. Check that the actual rent is more than the required rent.

Having used this quick approximation, if the property does not stack up, you can move on to the next one without wasting too much time. If, however, it looks like it does stack up well, it may be worth spending a little more time to work out properly the true cash flow to help you decide if you want to purchase it.

How much cash flow can I expect for each property?

This really depends on the purchase price and the rent that can be achieved which varies dramatically around the country. Very often I hear investors complain that investments just don't stack up where they live.

Whilst I would agree that it is possible that investments may not stack up exactly where you live, I would suggest that there

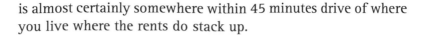

is almost certainly somewhere within 45 minutes drive of where you live where the rents do stack up.

Where I live in the West Midlands, a mid-terrace property with three bedrooms and two reception rooms may be worth £120,000 and would attract a rental income of £595 per month. If you had a 75% mortgage on this property, the mortgage advance would be £90,000. My rule of thumb would suggest that this would cost £450 per month in interest payments. The rent multiplier would suggest that the monthly costs would be approximately £562.50 (£450 x 125%). With a monthly rental of £595 this would provide a positive cash flow of approximately £35 a month which, frankly, is not a lot to get excited about.

At this monthly profit how many of these properties would you need to replace your monthly income? Probably more than you would care to own. With this kind of monthly profit, many people can't be bothered to invest in property probably because they forget about the long term benefits.

Yes we need the property to cover its costs in the short term and make positive cash flow for us, but it is for the long term benefits that we are investing. In 10 years time this property could have doubled in value from £120,000 to maybe £240,000.

We understand the long term benefits of property investing. How can we make the short term look more attractive? Well, there are a number of ways we can increase the cash flow from our property investments.

How about letting to a Local Housing Authority?

More and more landlords are deciding to let their properties to people claiming benefits because the rent that the Local Housing Authority (LHA) will pay for a property is often higher than the average market rent in the area.

The amount of rent that the LHA will pay depends on what the tenant is entitled to rather than the property itself. For example, a single mother with a few children of a certain age may be entitled to a three-bedroom house which will attract a higher LHA rate than a couple who want to rent the same house. A single mother may also make a great long term tenant as she may want to stay in your investment property long term so that her children can settle in the local school.

Some investors don't like the idea of letting to LHA tenants as they feel their house may get trashed. Whilst there are some undesirable LHA tenants, I have found that the vast majority of people on benefits are decent people who just don't happen to or can't work. I have some fantastic tenants who are on benefits.

With any tenants, whether they are on benefits or not, you do need to carry out your tenant referencing to check them out. A word of warning here! You may do a credit check on someone and they have a good job and a great credit score but something can happen in their life such as being made redundant or the breakdown of a relationship and suddenly they go off the rails and stop paying the rent. At least with an LHA tenant you know that they don't work and that the Government is essentially paying their rent!

Only you can decide if you want to rent to LHA tenants in some of your properties. I suggest as a minimum you should contact your local council to find out what the LHA rates are in your area. Often you can buy ex-council properties for very good prices and put LHA tenants into these properties and make great cash flow. Generally ex-council properties have good-sized rooms and so can be easy to rent in the right locations.

Boost your rental income with multi-lets

Instead of a single Assured Short-hold Tenancy (AST) contract, one of the best ways to get cash flow from your property is to rent it out room by room on a multi-let basis. If you rent out individual rooms in a property to students or young professionals, the combined rent will be much higher than the rent achieved if you rent the property to a family.

In the previous example we considered a £120,000 property which we could rent to someone for £595 per month. Instead of renting this property to a family, you could rent out the rooms to four different people. Remember, the property had three bedrooms and two reception rooms, one of which could be used as a bedroom, giving you four renting units. For this type of property, you would generally include in the rent the bills such as gas and electricity, community charge, etc. With a normal single AST rental contract, the tenants would be responsible for their own bills but in a shared house the rent is usually inclusive of utility bills and council tax. The rent you could charge each individual will vary based on the size of the room, facilities of the house and, of course, location of the property.

I have many of these multi-let properties which accommodate four to five individuals, where I achieve an average rent of about £350 per room per month. This means that each month I receive a total income for the property of about £1,750. After taking out the cost of the bills which is usually about £350 per month, I have over £1,400 in rental income, compared to £595 on a single AST contract. Take out the cost of the mortgage and I average between £500 to £700 positive cash flow every month from each of these houses, depending on the number of tenants. How many of these would you need to replace your income? You don't need to have 100 properties; just 10 would be more than enough for most people to be financially independent.

If you like the idea of renting out your properties on a multi-let basis to maximise your cash flow, there are a number of things you need to consider:

Property location: Location is always important when buying property, but particularly with a multi-let property. You need to make sure the property is in an area where your potential tenants would like to live. Things to consider will be public transport links, local facilities and amenities, proximity to their place of work.

The size of the rooms: In all of my rental properties I want to make sure that I can fit at least a queen size, if not a double bed into all of the bedrooms. For some reason, young professionals and students like to sleep in double beds, I don't know why! Then, where possible, we fit en-suite facilities into bedrooms making sure we still have enough room for wardrobes, chests of drawers and room to swing a cat.

The number of rooms: As all of the utility bills are included in the rent, it is important to make sure you have at least four rentable rooms per property to spread the cost of the monthly bills. I have found that with only three tenants in the property, the extra amount that I need to charge each tenant makes the rent uncompetitive in my local market. The more tenants you have, the further you have to spread the cost of the bills.

The quality of accommodation: Just because you are renting out your property on a room by room basis, don't think that you can provide sub-standard accommodation. Far from it; the quality of accommodation has to be high in order to attract your potential tenants. There is a lot of competition in the market but I always maintain that if you have good quality accommodation in the right location at the right price, you should always be able to find suitable tenants. All of my multi-let properties are set up to a very high standard. Many of the bedrooms have private en-suite facilities; all of the properties are renovated to a high standard; the properties all come with cable TV and there is broadband internet in every room.

HMO licensing

In July 2006, the government's legislation regarding houses in multiple occupation (HMO) came into force. This means that any property with five or more tenants on three or more floors is legally obliged to be licensed with the local council. The interpretation of the law regarding licensing has been left to local authorities, so the criteria do vary from council to council. For example, Swindon council in their infinite wisdom have decided that any property on three or more floors with just three tenants needs to be licensed as an HMO. It is important to check with your local council to ensure that you keep up to date with all their housing regulations.

If you are operating an HMO property which requires mandatory licensing, you need to contact your local council to obtain a license application form. The process is actually quite simple, even if rather time-consuming. You complete the forms and submit them with your application fee, which I have seen vary by anything from £500 to £1500 (which is usually for five years). At some point, your property will be inspected to make sure it meets all the relevant standards. Whether your multi-let property needs to be licensed or not, it still needs to adhere to the current safety standards regarding the fire doors, emergency exits and lights etc. I recommend you contact your local council to seek guidance to ensure that you are providing suitable safe accommodation for your tenants.

Planning permission for multi-lets

Not to be confused with mandatory HMO licensing, this is a totally different matter. In April 2010 the then Labour Government's Housing Minister introduced legislation designed to help local councils control the 'studentification' of certain areas. The Conservative Party had vowed to abolish this legislation if they came to power, which they did in May 2010 in a coalition with the Liberal Democrat party. We will have to see what actually happens, but at the time of writing I wanted to make you aware of this requirement.

If you convert a residential property to an HMO where three or more unrelated people live, you have to apply for planning permission for change of use. If the property was already used as an HMO before April 6th 2010 then you may not need to get the planning permission.

The best thing to do is to check with the planning department at your local council. At the time, I spoke to a number of councils around the country where I own property; some were adamant that they wanted to enforce the legislation and others were not so bothered.

First time buyer multi-let strategy

I am often asked by first time buyers how they can get on to the property ladder. My standard answer is usually that they should buy a property with a number of rooms, so they can rent out the spare rooms to their friends or other young professionals. This is how I purchased my very first property. I had graduated from the University of Birmingham in debt and with no job. Eventually, I secured a very good job at Cadbury Ltd in Birmingham and I decided that, rather than renting, I would love to buy my first property. As it was my own home I was able to obtain a 95% mortgage. I didn't have any deposit at all, so I needed to borrow the remaining 5% from a family member, for which I paid them interest. Although I didn't know it at the time, my first property purchase was in fact a no money down deal as the entire purchase was funded with other people's money. I then rented out the two spare rooms in my home to two of my friends who were still studying at university. This worked really well for me as their rent covered the cost of the mortgage, and I was just left to pay the household bills, which

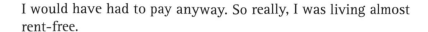

I would have had to pay anyway. So really, I was living almost rent-free.

I believe this is probably the best strategy that any young person can use to get on the property ladder. Property is now far more expensive than when I purchased my first home. However, it is easier to get finance now than it was when I first started to invest. A first time buyer can now obtain a mortgage, whereby a parent can be used as a guarantor or even the parent's income can be taken into account with some lenders. It is always best to check with your independent mortgage broker to find out what is possible right now.

It is more a case of the first time buyer being able to afford the mortgage. If they are renting out a few of the rooms in their property, they should be able to cover the cost of the mortgage. This then leaves the question of how they raise a deposit to purchase the property. My solution would be to borrow the deposit from someone such as a family member or friend who already owns a property. The property owner may have plenty of equity in their property. The first time buyer could approach the family member and suggest an opportunity for a family member to get involved in the property investment, by lending the first time buyer the deposit to buy the property.

Taking this strategy one step further, it is a great way for a young person to buy a property while they're still a student at university. Many parents purchase properties for their kids while they are studying at university, but they do it in the wrong way. Here is a great strategy to take advantage of the tax savings.

Student multi-let strategy

Accommodation for students at university can be very expensive. Many parents with children at university have realised that paying for university accommodation for three or four years is dead money. For this reason, many parents decide to purchase a student property to accommodate their children and their friends whilst they are at university. Instead of being a drain on resources, this can actually make money, as property in the right student locations always seems to go up in value, due to the high turnover and continual demand.

Most parents will release equity from their own home to raise a deposit for the investment property, which they purchase with a Buy to Let mortgage in their own name. Their children and their friends then become the tenants. Although this is a good strategy, it fails to take advantage of several tax benefits that would be achieved if the property was put in the student's name instead of the parents' name.

The parents would release equity from their own home in exactly the same way to raise a deposit, but rather than purchasing a buy to let property in their name, they would help their child purchase a residential property using a first time buyer mortgage. This scenario where the student is the owner of the property has several tax advantages:

1. The student will be able to receive rental income from the property and use their personal tax allowances to mitigate any IT liability. They will be able to earn £4,250 on the Rent a Room scheme and, in addition to this, a further £9,205 using their personal tax allowance (based on 2013-2014 tax allowances). This means they could earn over £13,000 in rental income and pay no tax on this revenue. If the property were in the parents' name any profits would be taxed at the parents' income tax level.

2. Once the student has finished university, they may decide to hold on to the property, or they may decide to sell. Any revenue generated from the sale of the property will be totally tax-free as this will have been the primary residence for the student. If the property

was in the parents' name, any profits would be subject to CGT.

If the student decides to hold on to the property, as the value increases they could re-mortgage it, to release the original deposit which can be returned to the parents. This is a far more tax-efficient way of doing it and it helps the student build their credit rating.

The buy to sell strategy

When I buy property I like to hold it for the long term. I don't really like to sell just to make some short term cash. However, when you are sourcing below market value properties, you will come across some properties that may not be suitable to rent out. Probably the market rents in the area may not be sufficient to support the Buy to Let mortgage and the location may not be suitable to let the property out on a multi-let basis.

Rather than walking away from the deal, it may be possible to buy the property at the discounted rate and sell it on at a higher price for a cash profit.

This can be a really good strategy to make you extra cash. Remember that if you sell any property other than your primary residence, you have to pay CGT on the profit. Many investors actually plan to sell at least one of their properties each year to take advantage of their annual capital gains allowance. Personally, I want to make sure that in any given year I always buy more properties than I sell, so that the net effect is that my portfolio is always growing in size.

The other consideration, of course, is the ease with which you will be able to sell the property. I believe it is always a risky strategy when the market is static or in decline. You may have to hold on to the property for a long time and may have to discount the price substantially in order to sell it. You do need to consider the market conditions at the time to see if this is an appropriate strategy.

I wanted to share this strategy with you so that you know what to do when we have the right market conditions. I am currently finding below market value properties and then selling them on to first time buyers and amateur investors, who do not expect discounts as large as I would want. If you are buying and flipping there are some tips you need to follow:

Make sure you get a big enough discount

To buy and flip a property, my rule of thumb is that you need to purchase it for at least 25% below the true market value. This is because to make any money you need to get a big enough discount to cover the purchase costs, sale costs, holding costs and allow for the property to be sold on to the end consumer at a small discount. I recommend you sell it at slightly less than the market value, to make sure that the price is competitive compared to all the other similar properties on the market at the same time. For example, if you were able to buy a property worth £160,000 for just £120,000, you would maybe put it on the market with an estate agent at £139,950 to sell it quickly.

Make sure you can cover the holding costs

The property may take a while to sell on the open market. Until it is sold you will have to cover all of the holding costs such as the interest payments on the mortgage, insurance, and maybe council tax etc. The longer it takes to sell the property, the higher your holding costs will be so you need to make sure you have enough cash flow to cover these holding costs.

Use a great estate agent

The time taken to sell your property depends partly on the quality of estate agent you use. Selecting the right estate agent is vital. You want an agent who is proactive and has lists of investors and buyers looking for the type of property that you have to sell. They should be able to advise you on the price at which you need to put the property on the market to achieve a quick sale. Make sure that you keep on top of them to find out what they are doing to sell the property for you. I usually work with estate agents with whom I already have a relationship, as I know they will work harder for me to sell the property. Don't try to beat them down on their selling commission; they need to be motivated to sell it for you. You may even want to offer them bonus commission for selling quickly.

Make the property appealing

When you buy a BMV property it can often look old and tired. To attract a buyer who is prepared to purchase the property at a good price, you need to make sure that the property looks desirable. Spending some money on cosmetic improvements should prove to be a worthwhile investment of your money. We have all seen the home improvement programs on television which show you how to prepare a house for sale. It is amazing what a difference a tidy-up and a fresh coat of paint can have on a property. You need to budget for any improvements and make sure you spend your money wisely. Places where you can add value to a property include the kitchen and bathroom. The general appearance of the property should be clean and tidy. Make sure any rubbish and debris is removed from the back yard and the front garden and ensure you maintain the gardens while the property is on the market. It is worth spending a few hundred pounds to dress the property with some colour pictures, mirrors and make sure it always smells nice with the use of plug-in air fresheners.

CASE STUDY: Thor Portess

I am now a professional property investor, making a very good living sourcing discounted properties in London, living my ideal lifestyle. But it was not always that way! I come from North Queensland in Australia where I grew up on a farm. After working in an underground mine for 8 long years, at the age of 27 I decided to go travelling, as all good Ozzies do!

After travelling in Europe for 6 months, to pay my way I started labouring for an Irish Shop-fitters and worked all around Ireland and Scotland whilst learning the building trade with them, for the next 2 years. I had a great time, but it was very hard work.

It was not until I came to England that it all changed for me. I attended Property Magic Live in October 2008, just as the recession ended Shop-fitting for me. I was so inspired, that I moved to London specifically to do property, as I thought I would learn the quickest here, in one of the economic capitals of the world. I recognised I needed to educate myself and, was fortunate enough to get a place on Simon Zutshi's 12 month, Property Mastermind Programme.

I quickly went on to purchase my first investment in East London in March 2009 for £128,000 when it was valued at £173,500. £45k equity in my first deal! I've since done 17 other Joint Ventures varying from packaging, buy & hold, buy to flip, Purchase Lease Options and Long Stop Completions.

For those investors, who think they can't get property deals in London, I thought I would share with you the details of one of my recent transactions:

The seven week flip!

In July 2010, Thomas, (one of my JV partners who I met on the Mastermind Programme) picked up a lead through an ex work colleague, for a 2 bed mid terrace in Wimbledon. An elderly Landlord in Wimbledon had been moved into a care home and the family needed to sell, to start paying for the nursing home. We met the family the day before they were to instruct an Agent to list the property. One agent had valued it at £430,000 and the other at between £365,000 and £375,000.

We were able to delay the listing, by offering to buy for cash and give them a definite sale, before they were going on vacation in September. They didn't want the hassle of having a sale that may have fallen through with a normal buyer. After some conversations, we negotiated a purchase price of £312,000. We had a deadline to complete in 7 weeks before the family went on holiday.

Plan A, was to find all of the cash to buy the property (which we did using cash investors and our own cash) and then to spend circa £60,000 on the property, by refurbishing and adding a loft conversion and a rear extension, all within permissable development (i.e. without the need for planning). After the work, we estimated we could easily sell for £ 430,000, maybe even £450,000, but of course nothing is guaranteed, particularly when it's 6 months away in a turbulent market place!

One of the Estate Agents with whom we viewed some properties to get an idea of comparables, viewed our property and said they thought they could find a buyer for us. We got the deal locked in with a Purchase Option and then started viewings. I met one of the prospective buyers by chance at the property, while taking some measurements for an architect. I showed her what we planned to do, if we didn't sell it beforehand. I explained the situation and said that we were happy to flip without doing any work, if someone could buy quickly. She liked the idea and decided to go ahead. We gave her 3 weeks to exchange and 5 weeks to complete with us, so we could meet our deadline.

Three weeks later, we simultaneously exchanged with the seller and also exchanged with our buyer. It was a hectic 3 weeks, as we had to prepare for both exit strategies, in case the 1st fell through and she decided not to exchange. We were busy getting drawings done, building quotes and speaking to the building inspector to get ready for the refurbishment development.

Fortunately, none of this was needed in the end, as we completed on our 7 week deadline at £312,000 and the same day completing with our buyer for £375,000. We made £43,000 between us and, also paid off some investors who we borrowed cash from.

Summary of the deal as follows:

- This lead came to a Joint Venture partner by word of mouth, at no cost to us.

- Value of the property before work £375k, after work £430k, with an agreed purchase price of £312,000.

- First plan was to refurbish for £60,000 and sell between £430k and £450k.

- Actually, we flipped in 7 weeks to a cash buyer, found by an estate agent, before refurbishment for £375k

- Profit of £43k, after paying all costs.

To make money doing flips, there are some things you have to do. First of all educate yourself. I highly recommend the Property Mastermind Programme. Then, you need to network with good people and tell everybody what you do. When you have a great deal it will go fast, if you don't act quickly. Be persistent and never give up. Most of my deals have had turning points in them, where they may not have gone to plan. But we kept pushing until the end. And finally always have two alternative exit strategies.

Cash for selling leads and deals

When you start to generate your own motivated seller leads you will no doubt come across a number of deals which represent great investment opportunities, but which don't fit your personal investment strategy. It is possible for you to make a very good income from selling leads that you do not want to other investors.

A number of the properties that I have purchased BMV have come from another investor, who specialises in sourcing leads. This investor spends a huge amount of money advertising to attract motivated sellers. Out of the hundreds of people who call him, every single month, he will discount many of them, because they are not true motivated sellers. However, from all the calls he receives, he will usually find at least a few sellers where there is, potentially, a good deal. Now of course, the investor will take some of the best deals for himself as one might expect, but often he will get a deal that is outside of his geographic area, so therefore he has no interest in purchasing it. These are some of the deals that he passes on to me and a few other selected investors with whom he is working. Some of the leads that he passed to me I purchased myself and some which are unsuitable for me are passed on to other investors. I pay this investor 2% of the purchase price (plus VAT) for every deal that actually goes through. I have a good relationship with him, whereby I only pay if the deal actually happens.

There is a great opportunity for you to make money in exactly the same way. The amount of money which you can generate will depend very much on the quality of the lead and how qualified it is. For example, if you had to pass on the name and address and property details of a motivated seller that you have not contacted, and so the lead may be unqualified, you may be able to sell this kind of lead on a website for somewhere between £50 and £150. However, the way to make money is to find qualified leads that you can pass on to other investors. A qualified lead is where you will have spoken to the seller, assessed the situation, provided a certain amount of background research, and maybe even agreed a price in principle with the seller. In short, you have done a lot of the legwork for another investor to whom you sell the deal.

Taking this one stage further, on a fully packaged done deal you could charge anywhere between 1% and 4% of the purchase price, depending on the nature of the deal. This could generate thousands of pounds for every deal package you supply to other investors. At this level of income, how many deals would you need to package for other investors each month to replace your current monthly income?

The very best way for you to make money selling these types of qualified leads and packaged deals, is to develop your own network of investors to whom you can pass qualified leads. You'd need to make sure your investors know what they are doing, and how to convert the leads into a completed property purchase so that you get paid. There is absolutely no point in you wasting a fantastic lead on an amateur investor who won't know what to do with it and may blow the deal because of their inexperience.

As part of my Property Mastermind Programme, we have an online forum where the Mastermind members can promote their unwanted deals to one another. Because everyone on the Mastermind Programme knows what they're doing, there is only a very small chance that the deal will fall over through lack of experience. There is also a high level of trust in the group that everyone will act ethically in their dealings with each other and the motivated sellers.

Summary of strategies to make cash flow:

1. Could you make more money letting to LHA tenants?

2. Can you multi-let your property?

3. Buy to sell in the right market conditions.

4. Selling deals to other investors.

Chapter 7:

You don't have to do everything on your own.

You need your own Power Team

One of the secrets to being a successful property investor is having a team of people around you who can help you achieve your goals. This group of individuals and companies will help you to achieve far more than you could possibly do on your own. Setting up a good power team is one of the first things you should do before even looking for investment opportunities. It's no good finding an amazing deal and then missing out on it, just because you can't move quickly enough.

With the correct power team in place, whenever you find a deal, you just pass the details on to your team and they will get on with it for you. Your role will then be to chase everyone to ensure the deal happens satisfactorily. You need to ensure that the different elements of your power team can work together effectively. They need to understand exactly what you're doing and the way you do it.

It is really important that the members of your team are very good at what they do. They should be doing their particular element every day. If you find that you have to explain to someone in your team what you require and they don't get it, then they do not have the required knowledge and so they are not right for you. Don't waste your time trying to educate your team. Instead find someone else who is already doing what you want them to do.

The best way to set up your power team is to network with other successful investors and get word of mouth recommendations. Occasionally, investors can be very protective of their power teams because they are worried that if they tell too many people about their great team, the individuals in the team may become overwhelmed with work and so their performance standards may slip. You'll also find that you will meet professionals who tell you that they can help you and do exactly what you want, but when it comes to the crunch, they don't know what they're doing. So if you are going to get your own team together, do expect there may be an element of trial and error until you find the right team. It may take you some time to get the right team in place, but once you have them you will be able to concentrate on finding the great deals.

Who should be in your power team?

Initially, you will start with a core power team consisting of the essential people you need to make the deals happen. With time you will probably develop an extended power team who will help you systematize the process and give you more free time to focus on what you want to do.

Your Core Power Team

This will include mortgage broker and solicitors. Let's consider each of these in turn.

Your mortgage broker: Probably one of the most important people in your power team. Your mortgage broker is your access to finance. Your mortgage broker needs to understand explicitly what you are doing. Don't assume that all mortgage brokers are the same.

My criteria for selecting a mortgage broker are as follows. They need to be:

- Fully independent with access to the entire mortgage market.

- Dealing with Buy to Let mortgages and re-mortgages on a daily basis.

- Able to respond quickly to your needs.

- Investing in property themselves.

Some mortgage brokers will charge you a fee and some will

work for you free of charge. Amateur investors often make the mistake of trying to save money by going to the cheapest supplier. Experience shows this is not always the best option. However, if you are dealing with the broker on a regular basis they should be prepared to negotiate their fee. The best way to find a good mortgage broker, as with most members of your power team, is through personal recommendation from other investors who use their services.

Your solicitors: You will need two different solicitors to complete your property purchase. One solicitor will represent you in the purchase of the property and a second, separate solicitor will represent the seller in the sale. I have had a number of experiences where the deal has almost fallen through because the seller's solicitor was just not very good. I cannot afford to risk this so I offer to cover the cost of the seller's solicitor, as long as the seller uses the solicitor that I recommend. The solicitor that I recommend will, of course, have to act in the best interest of the seller. However, I know the solicitor that I recommend has a good working relationship with the solicitor representing me and so I can ensure the transaction will happen in the required time.

My criteria for selecting solicitors are as follows. They need to be:

- Friendly and contactable with a good response rate.

- Proactive, rather than most solicitors who are reactive.

- Able to carry out all of the transactions over the phone and by e-mail for speed.

- Able to work with the other solicitors in an efficient manner.

- Cost-effective for the service they provide.

Your Extended Power Team

Over time, you will develop your extended power team which may include the following: estate agents, letting agents, builders, property finders and property coaches, to name just a few. Let's consider some of these:

Estate agents:

As discussed in Chapter 3, estate agents can be a great source of potential motivated sellers for you. I have a number of estate agents who call me first when they find the right kind of deal. In addition to sourcing property for you, the same estate agents can help you sell the properties which you want to buy and flip on. It is well worth investing the time to build up good relationships with the right kind of estate agents.

Letting agents:

Employing a good letting agent can save you a lot of time and hassle. Unfortunately, many letting agents aren't very good but if you know how to find them, there are some good ones out there. Letting agents can also be a good source of motivated seller leads for you because if any of their landlords decide to sell a property, the letting agents are often the first people to find out about it. If you have a good relationship with your agent this could be another source of leads for you. You may not require letting agents to manage a property for you, but they can be very useful in helping to find the tenants. It is not a good use of your time to manage your own properties.

Property finders:

As well as finding your own motivated seller leads, you may well have a number of other property investors and property finders who are out looking at deals for you. This is particularly useful if you're working full-time and just can't afford the time to do it yourself. You will have to pay them a fee but if it means you get to build up a property portfolio with very little effort, it can be well worth it.

Call answering service:

Whenever you are contacted by a motivated seller, you need to speak to them in person. If a seller goes through to your answer-phone, most of them will be reluctant to leave a message as they don't really know who you are. Rather than leaving a message, it is more likely that the seller will just move on to the next property problem solver, and you may have missed out on a potential deal. If you are constantly busy on your phone or unable to answer it during the day, you need to make a provision for someone else to answer on your behalf. Whoever answers the phone for you must have a script so they know exactly what to say and capture all the required information.

Builders:

If you are adding value to properties through renovation work, you will need professional builders to carry out the work for you. Remember, it is not worth your time doing this work yourself, so it's best to pay a professional to do it properly. The best way to build up a good relationship with your builder is to pay them promptly. Builders always seem to be chasing people for money, so if you pay them promptly in full, you will become one of their favoured clients, so that they may well prioritise your jobs over those of other people as they know they will get paid by you on time.

Handyman:

You may need someone to keep an eye on your properties and carry out small jobs of maintenance and repair. Having a local multi-skilled handyman who is available to attend to your properties at short notice can be really useful to you.

Property coach or mentor:

Once you get to a certain number of properties you may find it very difficult to talk to family and friends about what you're doing. They just won't understand it, and this is the point when

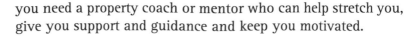

you need a property coach or mentor who can help stretch you, give you support and guidance and keep you motivated.

Now that we have considered the type of people you need in your power team, you may want to think about the gaps in your current team. Who else do you need in your team? How are you going to find them?

Widen your possibilities through joint ventures

To become a really successful investor you need to think bigger than, just what you can do on your own. Working with other investors in joint ventures can give you access to a greater number and variety of investment opportunities. A joint venture can give you:

- Access to knowledge and experience.

- Money to fund the project.

- Time to find great deals.

- Better networks of suppliers and contacts.

A joint venture makes the most of leverage, so that there is no limit to what you can achieve with the right joint venture partners. When you get a reputation of being very good at what you do, you will find that people will bring deals to you. One of the benefits that I gain from teaching other investors how to invest successfully is that I get the exposure to thousands of potential joint venture partners every year. Occasionally, investors bring great deals back to me that they feel they cannot do on their own and so they want to use my expertise to make sure the deal happens. This works very well for all the parties involved.

Joint venture partners generally fall into two categories. You have the people who are 'cash rich and time poor' and the people who are 'time rich but cash poor'. Which category do you fall into? Maybe you are reading this book and thinking that you are both 'cash poor and time poor!' Don't worry, you can still do deals but you just need to think smart and work very creatively.

CASE STUDY: Dick Dabner

I have been an entrepreneur all my life and I was delighted when my son Peter joined the family business when he left school. We worked hard for 10 years together in the glass industry, expanding into manufacturing and retail. In the late 1990s we had four properties between us, one investment property each and the homes in which we each lived.

One day in 2002, going through the glass business figures after a particularly tough period of trading, it occurred to us that we had done better from the capital growth gained in the four properties than we had in the past 12 months working 60 hours a week in our 'day jobs', and the properties had taken only a few hours of management all year.

We made the decision to close down the glass business and concentrate on property full time. At that point, we had bank overdrafts and personal guarantees from the business that needed to be repaid, so we were highly motivated to start on property because we were determined to repay what we owed as quickly as possible.

We sold two properties to repay some debt and had the third property up for sale, but then we did a property course and learned that we could refinance the remaining two properties which would leave us with enough to put down the deposit on a small one-bed flat, which we bought with a Buy to Let mortgage.

We purchased this flat below market value and did a 'makeover' type of refurbishment, making sure that we 'added value', establishing the principle of making money by using this strategy. We knew that other flats in good order locally were selling for £120,000 - £130,000.

Our business plan was basic: buy for £92,000 and finish the refurbishment for less than £8,000, keeping the total to less than £100,000. We then had the flat re-valued and took another mortgage to refinance. It was surveyed and the new valuation came back at £125,000. We had made £25,000 of equity in a few weeks!

Peter had been looking for other properties with which we could use the same strategy, and had been offered both the flat next door and the flat opposite so we agreed to buy both at £93,000 each. We had no money of our own to expand and buy these properties, but we knew that there was another £50,000 waiting for us, as long as we could come up with the funds to buy these other two flats.

We started to speak to friends and family, telling them about what we were doing, and we soon found our first two joint venture business partners, who were prepared to put up the money in return for an interest rate or a share of the profit, with the promise that if it all went to plan, there was more money available.

This gave us the confidence to buy the two flats, which we could sell after refurbishing them. They were surveyed at £124,000 and £135,000 respectively and we were able to repay our investors including their profit.

We had made some money and, more importantly, we had also established the two principles that have worked for us ever since, no matter what the market conditions are: interest payment or profit share. As long as we find joint venture partners, identify good deals and add value to the property, we can make money for ourselves and for our investors whether the market is going up, down or sideways!

Our latest joint venture project was the purchase of a semi-detached property on a large plot with a workshop. The seller was in financial difficulty and the property was about to be repossessed. The property, which was on the market for £325,000, had been sold twice, only for the sale to fall through both times. We spotted the massive development opportunity for the site and decided to see if we could help this seller. We agreed a purchase price of £250,000 and stepped in to stop the repossession.

We managed to get a lock-out agreement which meant we could get into the property before exchange to do a simple refurbishment and also start the planning application. We then exchanged contracts on the condition that the deposit was used to clear the arrears, to make sure the property did not get repossessed. We had a delayed completion which gave us more time to get the planning approval.

We achieved planning permission to convert the semi-detached property into two x two-bed flats (worth £330,000), the workshop into a two-bed house (worth £240,000), and to build a pair of semi-detached properties on the plot (worth £300,000 each). This means the total development value of the site is £1.17m. One of our JV partners put in about £400,000 for the building work. After all the costs, our profit from this one purchase will be about £300,000 which we will split with our JV partners.

Now we have an established portfolio with a good rental income stream, and we are able to use this to pay interest to JV partners so that we can continue to expand.

We always pay far more than the banks, so that we find more new investors and most of them become long term joint venture partners. We know that, with their help, we can undertake far more projects in property than we could ever do on our own, and that way everybody wins.

Since discovering the power of working with other people, I have continued to expand my knowledge and experience in property by investing in my own education. Many of the strategies I now use for finding properties to buy and for structuring deals, have come directly or indirectly from participating in the Property Mastermind Programme and simply following the course and taking action in line with my goals. This has enabled me to prosper despite the adverse financial climate and I believe that joint ventures will provide continuing success in the future.

Elements of successful joint ventures

For a joint venture to work you have to select the right partners. First of all, each partner needs to bring something different to the partnership. It is really important to have an open and honest relationship. You should always start with clear, simple documents that outline how the partnership will work. You need to understand who is responsible for what in the partnership. As part of this agreement, you need to have a clear exit strategy, so you know exactly how and when the partnership will finish. You should also consider scenario analysis and contingency planning just in case things don't go to plan.

How to use your equity at no cost to you

I regularly meet investors who tell me they have no money to invest. Very often, after some questioning we discover that actually they do have plenty of money to invest, if they use the equity in their own home. The problem here is that many amateur investors do not want to use the equity from existing property for two reasons. First of all, they think it may be a risk, and secondly they recognise that there is a cost to do this and may be concerned about funding that cost.

Releasing equity from your own property is a great way to raise funds to invest in property and there are ways you can do it at no cost to you. Before I explain this idea, I must remind you that I'm not a regulated financial adviser. This does not constitute financial advice, I am merely suggesting some possibilities to you.

Imagine you own a property that has at least £100,000 of equity which you could release. At an interest rate of 6% this would cost you approximately £500 per month in interest. A useful rule of thumb to remember is that for every £20,000 of equity you release, it will cost you £100 per month in interest at an interest rate of 6%. Assume you meet another investor with whom you develop a good relationship. You may decide to go into a joint venture partnership on a project with them. You could lend the joint venture partner £50,000, which would be half of the money you have released. If you were to charge your partner an interest rate of 1% per month on this borrowed money they would have to pay you £500 per month interest. This interest payment you receive on the £50,000 they are borrowing from you will be enough to cover your interest on the entire £100,000 of borrowing. This means that you will have the remaining £50,000, which you can use to invest with the assurance that the cost of borrowing the money is covered by someone else.

The person who borrows the money also gets a great deal because it is far easier to borrow from a private individual than it is to borrow from a bank or lending institution. Of course, you need to pick your partner carefully, as you would not want to lend your money to just anybody. Make sure you have your agreement documented for future reference.

How to find a suitable joint venture partner

There are potential joint venture partners all around you! They could be family, friends or other investors. Some of those people may not know that they are your potential JV partners, at the moment, because they do not fully understand what property investing can do for them.

One of the first things you should do is to educate them. This may not be easy if you are new to investing yourself as they may think "What do you know about property"? A simple step would be to give them a copy of this book and tell them that you found it really interesting and think they will too. As long as they read it and you follow up, they may well be more inclined to have a discussion about how you could work together.

When you are looking for a potential joint venture partner, you need to consider what you have to offer, what you require and what is really important to you. Once you have worked this out, you need to look through your network of investors to identify a suitable partner – someone who has what you need and who needs what you have.

When you meet a potential partner, you need to find out what is really important to them. This is why it's important to network with other investors and build quality relationships. Once you have identified a suitable partner, you need to consider the type of deals in which you both want to be involved. I usually look at each joint venture proposal on its own individual merits. I decide if I want to get involved and then promote it out to suitable partners who I already know will be interested in that type of venture. I consider all the potential partners, and decide who I think would be best to get involved in that particular project, and then we set up a deal that is a WIN/WIN solution to both of us.

CASE STUDY: Gavin Barry

I have been a property investor for more than ten years now investing predominantly in Liverpool and specialising in HMO and LHA property.

In 2001, I decided I wanted to get into the property industry. After much research, I came to the conclusion that Liverpool offered the best long term potential in terms of capital growth and letting potential. In early 2003, I decided to drop everything I was doing in London and move to Liverpool, to set up a small residential development company, specialising in sourcing land and obtaining planning permission, renovating houses and splitting large houses into flats. My initial strategy was to sell everything I purchased. In 2007, I decided to alter my strategy and focus more on buy to hold strategy and build a large portfolio which would provide a pension in later life.

I decided to focus on student property and other multi-let properties, such as young professional house-shares and large houses split into self contained units, where rents can be maximised and returns can be significantly more substantial than single lets.

I currently have a portfolio of more than 60 properties, my own letting agency and separate maintenance company.

I first met Simon Zutshi in 2007 and considered doing the Mastermind programme, but back then, I couldn't commit to the dates and so decided to leave it. I met Simon again in 2010 and decided the time was right for me to do the course. As I said to Simon at the time, I wanted to get to the next level in terms of property investing, I wanted to learn more about sourcing and packaging deals for other investors and I wanted to learn about Option deals. My goal was to think big, focus on bigger deals and, leverage my time through strategic joint venture opportunities.

I have agreed a new joint venture partnership with a local builder, which will focus on local development and investment opportunities primarily in the student and HMO market – my role is to source the opportunity, arrange the development funding and re-finance once the development is complete. Once it is complete, my management company will let and manage the property, in addition to my maintenance company carrying out the maintenance.

One of the deals I have sourced recently for my new JV Company is a portfolio of four properties: two student houses, a large house split into six flats and a mixed use building with commercial on the ground floor, which I intend to move my letting agency into, once complete. The residential accommodation above, we will convert into student accommodation.

The vendor was a tired landlord looking to retire, who I met through a networking event I attend regularly. The properties had been in his portfolio a long time and he had very little debt on these particular properties. We agreed a deal where we would buy the two student houses and the block of six flats immediately, in cash and re-finance with commercial lending (after we split the title on the block of six flats and increased the value even more). We also agreed, we would exchange on the commercial mixed-use property and, gain access to carry out the refurbishment to the residential accommodation, before completing on the property, based on the higher valuation. All the properties were purchased with a 35% discount to current market value.

Summary of the deal as follows:

- Deal sourced from a motivated landlord met at a property network meeting.

- Portfolio value worth £1.3M, purchased 35% BMV.

- Purchased cash and re-financed with commercial finance, so no money left in.

- £400k equity with a substantial surplus cash flow each month, sufficient to pay down the loan in 15 years.

In summary since the start of the Mastermind course I have acquired property in excess of £2.2m for my own portfolio, sourced and packaged 12 properties in excess of £1m for other investors, which have generated nearly £95k in fees and profit. I have an Option deal on a property worth 700,000 Euros in Italy and, to top it all off, Simon explained a very useful scheme to us in the first workshop, which enabled me to claim back income tax paid from the last two years and generate enough capital allowances to ensure I won't have a tax bill for the next couple of years.

The most important lesson for me, however, through the course was learning to think big and the importance and value I put on my time which, as a result, I now have a structure and team in place to take advantage of many opportunities at any given time.

What should be in a joint venture agreement?

I'm often asked this question, but the reality is that you can make it anything you want, as long as it works for all the parties involved. I think it is important to have the agreement in writing, as there is a danger that there could be confusion in the future around a verbal agreement. The best advice I would give you is to keep it simple and straightforward. Basically, you need to include some information about the project outline and objectives. You need to detail the inputs from each partner, the timescales and deadlines involved. You also need to consider the financial arrangements and cash flow requirements of the project, as well as the expected returns, profit share and risk analysis. This might sound like a lot of detail but it could easily be covered on one sheet of A4 paper.

In conclusion to this chapter, you don't have to do everything on your own. You must value your time and remember that people with a rich mindset will spend their money to save time. I recommend that you focus on the things that you enjoy and that you are good at, and delegate all the other tasks to someone else who can do them better than you. With this in mind, who can you get to help you?

Chapter 8:

The best investment you can make!

Invest in yourself

Investing time and effort in your own education and personal development is the best investment you will ever make. The knowledge and skills you gain through education will stay with you for the rest of your life. For the majority of the population, the only education they get is the formal education they receive at school, college or even university. Unfortunately, this traditional form of education does absolutely nothing to teach you the fundamentals of life about money, finance and investing. Most people learn the hard way by making mistakes, which is a very expensive way to learn. A far easier, quicker and cheaper way to learn is from someone else who has already become successful, someone from whom you can learn from their success, and also from their mistakes.

Since 1999, I have spent a fortune on my own personal development and ongoing education. I'm constantly looking to improve myself, my skills and expertise. I believe you never stop learning, if only you are open to it. Without appearing to sound arrogant, I know that I'm very knowledgeable in the area of residential property investing. I have well over a decade of experience. I've made a lot of money, but also made a lot of mistakes. However, I don't claim to know it all. I am still learning and, because I'm involved in property investing every day, I learn something new every day. I'm always looking to learn from other successful investors and improve on what I do. I've noticed that the most successful people are also the most open-minded. I have coached and trained many thousands of investors since 2003 and, I have observed that some of the hardest people to teach are often those who have some experience. Sometimes, due to their experience they believe they know it all. A little knowledge can be a dangerous thing. It is very frustrating when someone says or thinks "I know" because they are closing down their mind to new possibilities and opportunities.

The point is, why would you want to learn the hard way, wasting your time, money and effort, when you can easily learn from someone else who has already been successful and can show you how to avoid the mistakes that most investors will make? I think one of the problems is that most people are not prepared to put the time, effort or money into educating themselves. I must admit, I was very sceptical, before I got into personal development. I remember my first exposure to personal development when I was about 24 and I wasn't very impressed. I was in a friend's car on a journey from Birmingham to London. As it was his car and he was driving, he insisted that we listen to his new Anthony Robbins personal development cassette tapes. I would rather have listened to the radio, but I didn't really mind and I suppose I was a little bit curious. I only half listened as I think I probably dozed off, but I just did not get it at the time. I think my friend got more of a reaction from me when he told me how much he had paid for this personal development audio pack ... £50! I could not believe it! £50 seemed like a lot of money to me at the time. I remember thinking to myself 'Why would anyone spend £50 on a set of tapes?' It's amazing how people change. Five years later, I spent almost £1,000 to go on my first business training seminar.

Nowadays, I think nothing of spending thousands of pounds to go on a seminar, sometimes even travelling to the other side of the world, because I know if I get just one good idea, it will be time and money well invested. I am selective about which seminars or courses I attend, but each year I commit to spending a certain amount of income and time developing myself further. I really enjoy learning, growing and stretching my thinking to help me perform at a higher level. I understand the value of paying for information and expertise. Last year I paid £7500 + Vat for one day of consulting with a business expert. The value I received from that one day was massive. People are happy to pay me £5000 a day to help them on a one to one basis with specific property advice, because I always give them 10 times more value than they pay me.

I am confident that, if for any reason I were to lose everything, I would be able to get back to where I am now much quicker, faster and easier than I did the first time, because I know exactly what to do this time and, maybe more importantly, what not to do. How about you? Are you investing enough in yourself? Do you have the skills and knowledge you need to be a successful property investor?

What skills do you need to be a successful investor?

Mental attitude: I firmly believe that you can have all the skills, knowledge and strategies in the world, but these are useless if you don't have the right investor's mindset. To be a successful investor you need to have the right attitude and self-belief that you can achieve anything you put your mind to. Most investors think that investing is all about the strategies and techniques you use. I personally believe that the strategies are 20% and your attitude and mindset are 80% of what it takes to be a really successful investor.

Positive outlook: Are you generally a positive or a negative person? I know we all go through phases, and sometimes we have bad days, but I promise you it is easier to achieve what you want if you're positive and looking for the possibilities rather looking for negatives and what can't be done. You get what you think about and focus on. As a property problem solver, you need to be very creative, with a solution-focused outlook. There is always a way. Your role is often to solve problems by finding solutions that other people cannot see.

Listening skills: The best way to help a motivated seller is to ask them what they want and listen to what they tell you. As simple as this sounds all too often, I hear of investors who talk at motivated sellers rather than talking with them. Building rapport and a trusting relationship is absolutely critical if you want to help these people and secure a good win/win deal. You need to become good at asking questions and, listening to the answers to make sure you really understand the situation and find the best possible solution for you and the motivated seller.

Research skills: Whenever you find a potential motivated seller lead, you need to act very quickly. Before you move on any deal, you need to quickly assess if it will work for you. Research is really important. You need to be able to determine the value of a property, the rental potential and realistic rental income that it might achieve. Luckily, it is extremely easy and quick to do this with the use of the internet and a telephone. In just ten minutes, you can obtain a realistic valuation that a chartered surveyor would also arrive at. You can use this information to support your estimated value during the survey.

Numerical skills: property investing is all about the numbers and return on your investment. You need to be able to work out if a deal stacks up or not. Luckily, you don't have to do this in your head or on the spot, but you do need to understand the numbers upon which you will base your investing decisions.

Negotiation skills: As I will always maintain throughout this book, you need to come up with a solution that is a win/win for both you and the seller. You need to be ethical and make sure that you do not take advantage of the seller's situation. Having said this, the deal has to work for you otherwise there is no point doing it. Remember, this is a business. In most motivated seller purchases there is some scope for negotiation. The level of your negotiation skills can dramatically impact the profitability of your business.

Self Discipline: To be successful we sometimes need to push ourselves and do things outside of our comfort zone. It can be very easy to use excuses as to why we have not done something, but really it just comes down to being disciplined and focused on what you want. We may need to make some short term sacrifices in order to achieve and enjoy long term benefits.

Having the discipline to do something each day to move you towards your goals will have a massive positive impact on your results.

Persistence: This is probably one of the most important skills you can develop. Investing in property is not easy. There are lots of challenges and obstacles you will need to overcome. Unfortunately most people give up far too easily, often just before they achieve the results they are looking for. You need to keep going and remember if other people have been successful and found a way there is no reason why you can't do the same.

Looking at your current skills set compared to the skills required to be a successful property problem solver, where do you feel that you may need to improve your skills? What can you do to improve your skills?

Remember, you don't have to be good at everything. You can get other people to help you in areas in which you are not so strong. Working with other people is much smarter than doing it on your own, which can be very lonely.

The smart way to educate yourself

Now that we have recognised the need to constantly improve yourself and develop your skills, knowledge and experience; there are several ways in which you can achieve this. You need to select the method(s) that best fit with your time and personal requirements. Here are a few ideas for you:

Networking: There are now many very good, specialist networking groups for property investors. Attending these events on a regular basis is one of the best ways to develop your knowledge by mixing with and learning from other successful investors. This is the main reason I founded the Property Investors Network (pin) back in 2003. I recognized the incredible value that I had personally gained by learning from and networking with other successful investors. Networking is a low cost way of gaining knowledge in terms of financial requirement, but it does require some time, effort and dedication from you.

The more investors you know and the bigger your network, the more opportunities you will become aware of. There are property investor groups all over the UK. I suggest you use the internet to find a group near to where you live or work and start visiting on a regular basis. This is also a great way to keep yourself motivated and on track. Property investing can be lonely sometimes, especially if your friends and family don't really understand what you do. You need to be around like-minded people who can give you support, encouragement and advice. We hold property investor network meetings in major cities around the UK every month. To find out about your local pin meeting you can visit www.PinMeeting.co.uk

Educational seminars and courses: There are a number of individuals and companies in the UK who provide property investing education. Some of them are better than others and it is up to you to decide which is best for you. Seminars are a great way for you to learn a lot of information very quickly. Although you often have to pay to attend these seminars; the knowledge that you gain will make the investment of time and money very worthwhile.

To be honest, given enough time and research, you could probably discover for yourself most of the information that you will learn on a seminar. However, the main reason you attend a seminar is to obtain a lot of information, compressed into a very short amount of time, instead of having to spend months reading books, looking on the internet and speaking to other investors. You need to start valuing your time and recognise when you are spending time and when you are investing time. This comes back to mental attitude. Amateur investors with a poor mindset will spend their time to save money, whereas investors with a rich mindset will always spend their money to save time. Rich people realise that time is their most valuable asset.

One tip that I would give you is, that you need to make sure the presenter who is sharing their knowledge is actively investing themselves. Do they have practical experience or are they just teaching you theory that they have learnt from a book? Make sure they are 'walking their talk'. Also be wary of the companies who run seminars to get you all excited about property investment and at the end of the seminar want you to sign up at the back of the room to buy investments there and then. Now, these may be perfectly good investment opportunities, but how do you know that? You should never buy any property investment just because you see other people buying it. You always need to do your own research before you decide to buy anything. That does not mean you should take a long time to decide, it just means you need to do your research thoroughly and quickly to decide if the opportunity is right for you.

Home study: If you can't seem to make the time to attend live seminars, or the dates and locations just don't work for you, then home study could be a good solution. There are plenty of DVDs, Audio CDs and home study courses that you can buy, which means you can fit learning in around your lifestyle. If you spend a lot of time travelling to and from work rather than listening to the radio, you could use this time productively by listening to an educational CD.

Coaches or mentors: Reading books or attending seminars to learn how to invest in property is pointless unless you put your knowledge into practice. One of the best ways of doing this is to have a coach who will support you, help you to take action and hold you to account. Your coach should be someone who is more experienced than you and can add value to your investing, help you to grow and expand your knowledge. Your coach must have a proven track record and ideally should be recommended to you by another successful investor. Some of the most successful graduates from my Mastermind Programme have gone on to become property coaches in their own right.

So what are your next steps?

The purpose of this book is raise your awareness of what is possible, inspire you to change your life for the better, whilst helping other people solve their property problems.

I sincerely hope that you have enjoyed reading this book, found it inspirational and have learnt a great deal from it. When I sat down to write this book, my objective was to share with you some of the incredible learning that I've gained through teaching the motivated seller purchase strategies to my Property Mastermind Programme delegates. Having just read through the manuscript myself, I now realise that although I have explained the basic principles, I've only just scratched the surface of what I could teach you based on my experience.

I have deliberately kept the strategy explanations as simple as possible, and I believe that you have enough information to decide if the motivated seller strategy is appropriate for you. Personally, I believe that this strategy is perfect for anyone who is interested in building a significant portfolio in a relatively short amount of time. Knowledge alone is useless; you need to put your knowledge and skills into action.

Further learning with me

I would like to share with you, details of how I believe I can help you further on your property investing journey. I want to hold your hand and help to make the journey smoother, quicker and more enjoyable than if you try to do it on your own.

So for your information, here is the further training and support we can help provide for you.

Property Investors Network (pin) – Monthly evening seminars

The purpose of pin is to provide a support environment in which you can continue to learn more about successful property investing. Every month we host evening network seminars in a number of cities around the country. There are two fundamental aspects to these monthly meetings: 1) Networking and 2) Education. These events give you a great opportunity to meet, learn from and network with other successful investors. Each month, we cover a different investing topic in the educational seminars. I am delighted to say that we consistently attract some of the top UK property investing experts to speak at our events.

Doors open for these events at 6.00 p.m. with informal networking. The educational seminar runs from 7.00 p.m. until about 9.00 p.m. after which informal networking continues. I recommend you come along to your local pin meeting. You need to reserve your place in advance online.

All of the monthly events, dates and locations are listed here: www.PinMeeting.co.uk

As my gift to you, if you have never been to a pin meeting, I would like to invite you to attend your first local pin meeting as my guest, completely free of change. Normally entry is just £20 per person, but if you follow the easy steps outlined below, there will be no charge for your first visit.

- Go to wwwPinMeeting.co.uk

- Choose which pin meeting you would like to attend.

- Click "Book with a Voucher code".

- Enter your name, email address and mobile number.

- Enter "propMagic"

- Click "Click here to book your place now" button.

- Your name will be added to the guest list and an email confirmation will be sent to you.

The Ultimate Property Investors Bootcamp - audio programme

This best-selling study at home audio programme provides a solid foundation for anyone who is serious about investing in property. Guest speakers on this programme, include some of the top property investing experts in the UK and all of my personal power team. With over 12 hours of audio material, this is an incredibly detailed programme which covers the following topics:

- Why you should be investing in property!

- Planning your strategy and conducting research.

- Fundamentals of property investing.

- Understanding Finance and taxation.

- How to profit from property options.

- Benefits of networking and Joint Ventures.

- Buying property from Estate Agents and Auctions.

- Buying property from motivated sellers.

- Letting your property.

- Maximizing the rent on your property.

- Advanced Investing Strategies.

- How to take you investing to the next level.

For full details of exactly what you'll learn on this home study course visit this website now:

www.ThePropertyBootCamp.com

All of our products come with a 100% money back guarantee. If you don't think that this is the best property investing course you've heard, simply return the entire package to us within 30 days and receive your money back in full.

This is such a good fundamental property investing programme that everyone who comes on the Property Mastermind Programme receives the DVD version of this course as part of their Brain Transplant Pack.

Property Magic Live DVDs

Inspired by the success of this book, every two years we organise a two-day Property Magic Live weekend seminar.

This is where we share the latest property investing strategies combined with inspirational case studies, to help you become a more successful investor. To find out about the next Property Magic Live event or to buy the DVD highlights from previous events visit this website:

www.PropertyMagicLive.co.uk

Individual coaching and mentoring

Property Investors Network now offers a one to one private coaching service to help support you and hold you to account. The coaches are some of the most successful graduates from the Property Mastermind Programme whom I have personally selected and trained to be property investment coaches.

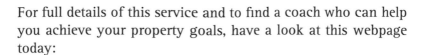

For full details of this service and to find a coach who can help you achieve your property goals, have a look at this webpage today:

www.PinMeeting.co.uk/Coaching

Property Investing Quick Start – one-day seminar

I have created a special one-day seminar designed to teach you what you need to know to start buying property well below market value, right now. This seminar expands on some of the ideas shared in this book and explains exactly how to put the theory into practice.

By attending this Property Investing Quick Start Seminar you will learn the following:

- 28 reasons why vendors may be motivated to sell their property up to 40% below market value.

- 20 strategies to find motivated sellers, including the quickest way to access them within 24 hrs without spending a penny.

- How to deal with motivated sellers so that they want to sell to you instead of any other investors.

- The 5 magic words to prove to sellers that you want to help them find an ethical win/win solution to their problem.

- The negotiation strategy that could get an extra 20% discounted off the BMV price.

- How to quickly evaluate a deal to decide if you should buy it or not.

- How to use "momentum investing" to recycle your deposit which means that you can quickly build up your property portfolio.

- How you can use other people's money as deposits if you run out your own source of finance.

- Introduction to how to use Purchase Lease Options to control and profit from property that you don't own.

- How to plan your exit strategy to minimise the tax liability and maximise your profit

Full details of this one day quick start seminar, along with dates and locations, can be found on this website: www.PropertyInvestingQuickStart.co.uk

The Mastermind Accelerator 3 day workshop

This is an advanced three-day, residential workshop in which we work through my Property Investing Strategy Flow Chart and all the associated investing strategies.

This workshop is designed for the more advanced investor and is highly recommended for anyone who is considering the joining the full Property Mastermind Programme.

Having spent three days with me (learning more than most investors learn in three years) you will subsequently know that the Property Mastermind Programme is perfect for you.

As usual there is a 100% money back guarantee to ensure that you have nothing to risk and everything to gain.

Full details of this advanced 3-day workshop, along with dates and locations can be found here: www.MastermindAccelerator.co.uk

The Property Mastermind Programme

I have already mentioned my Property Mastermind Programme throughout this book and, so now would be an appropriate time to tell you how the programme may be of benefit to you.

I have been teaching other people how to successfully invest in property since 2003. Then one day in 2006, I was thinking about my business and made a radical decision: I decided that I wasn't going to run any more property investing seminars. This was a big decision because I really enjoyed speaking and teaching other people how to become financially independent, but I found myself becoming increasingly frustrated. Despite getting fantastic feedback from everyone who experienced my training, I was aware that there were a percentage of people who just didn't take action! I found this very frustrating and thought that maybe somehow it was my responsibility and so stopped teaching to concentrate on my own investing.

During that period I made a lot of money in property, but to be honest after 6 months I was bored. I then had a sudden realization, that it was the teaching and helping other people that I was passionate about, far more than investing. To me investing is just a vehicle to give me the financial independence to spend my time doing what I really love, which is speaking and teaching.

I made a decision that from then onwards, I only wanted to work with serious investors who were going to take action on the valuable information I had to share with them.

After months of planning and research I came up with a blueprint for the Property Mastermind Programme. The initial idea came from the Mastermind principle, which Napoleon Hill talks about in his classic book "Think and Grow Rich". With the help of my team and some of the UK's top property investing experts, we put together an outstanding year-long property investing programme, unique in the market, where it would be almost impossible not to succeed given all the support provided and accountability.

Our aim was to help anybody build a £1m property portfolio and achieve a £50,000 income in just 12 months. With property values as they are today, a £1m property portfolio on its own is not that difficult, but the real challenge is the £50,000 income. Is this really possible? Absolutely! Since the very first Property Mastermind Programme back in April 2007, and on all the subsequent programmes to date, we have had delegates who have smashed this target of £1m in property and a £50,000 income, sometimes in a lot less than 12 months, often from a standing start and with no money at all.

Has everyone been this successful? No! not everyone. Some people take a few years to achieve these sorts of results. As part of the Property Mastermind Programme, there is an accountability system to help support everyone and hold them to account.

Each year we start two, 12-month Property Mastermind Programmes, one in April and one in October, with a maximum of 60 investors on each programme. We have an impressive track record of results achieved by both novice and experienced investors. Have a look at some of the success stories for yourself at:

www.Property-Mastermind.com/CaseStudies

The Property Mastermind Programme consists of eight key elements specifically designed to help you gain maximum benefit.

1) The Brain Transplant Pack

The Property Mastermind Programme has been designed for both new investors and experienced investors alike. Understandably, all of the delegates will be at different levels of knowledge, experience and confidence before they start the programme, so the first thing we do is to help everyone get up to speed and be able to start from the same point. To achieve this, all participants receive the Brain Transplant Pack before the first workshop. This big pack of detailed information contains some of the very best property investing seminars I have run over the last few years in written, audio and DVD format, as well as some classic personal development programmes. If you were to purchase these products individually it would cost you almost £10k, but you get them for free as a delegate on the Property Mastermind Programme. This gives you a solid base of property investing knowledge on which we build in the monthly advanced workshops.

2) Monthly Advanced One-Day Workshops.

These are a fundamental part of the Property Mastermind Programme. At these advanced one-day events, you will experience an exponential growth in your knowledge, understanding and confidence thanks to the Mastermind principle and, the input of everybody in the group. Networking and working together as a team will enable you to achieve far more than working on your own. We encourage delegates to share their successes and their learning to benefit the rest of the group.

Over the 12-month period there are 10 advanced workshops, one every month with the exception of August and December. The content of each workshop is different and builds on the previous one. The content is constantly adapted and updated to account for changes in the property market.

It is really important that you commit to attend as many of these as possible. However, if you do happen to miss one or two, you can catch up by listening to the MP3s of the workshop that are made available to all of the delegates a week after each event.

By the end of each workshop, you will have a clear focus of exactly what you need to do before the next workshop, and a priority order in which your tasks need to be completed. There is an accountability system to make sure you take action and receive the maximum benefit from the learning experience.

Currently, delegates on the Property Mastermind Programme are from all over the UK and overseas; so, for ease of access, all of the workshops are currently held at a hotel at the Birmingham NEC, just next door to Birmingham International Airport, Birmingham International train station and the M42.

3) The Portfolio Building Portal

This is an incredibly useful private online forum, which helps the Mastermind members to keep in touch on a daily basis. It is a great source of information for any questions you may have or assistance you need from other members of the group, as well as graduates from previous Mastermind Programmes, who still have access to the forum. It's also a great place to find motivated seller leads and deals, being offered by other Property Mastermind members.

If you would like to have a sneak preview of behind the scenes in our private forum, you can have a look at the short online video at this website:

www.Property-Mastermind.com/ForumDemo

4) Property Mastermind Life Line

This element of the programme is designed to give you continued learning and direct access to me through monthly group coaching webinars. Each month, I host at least one webinar, when you can ask me any questions you want. In these online sessions, we summarise the information from the previous workshop and I coach you through any challenges you may have. These calls will help you to keep motivated between the advanced workshops. For your chance to experience a free

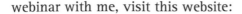

webinar with me, visit this website:

www.AskSimonZutshi.com

5) Your Mastermind Power Team

To be a successful investor you need to have the right team around you. As a delegate of the Property Mastermind Programme, you will have that team from day one, which means you don't have to waste your time or money finding your own team. On the advanced workshops, you will be introduced to the solicitors, mortgage brokers, property tax specialists, in fact all of my property power team whom I personally use to facilitate my property investing. Of course you do not have to use my team, you can use anyone you want, however we have set up a team ready for you that works.

We also show you how to systematize your lead generation and handling system, so that even if you have a full time job, you can make the Property Mastermind Programme work for you.

6) Lead Exchange and Joint Venture System

Using the online forum you will be able to offer your unwanted leads to other Mastermind members and purchase leads direct from them. By working as a group, you can have all of the Mastermind delegates out there looking for deals for you.

We always have a variety of different investors on the Mastermind Programme. Some of the investors are cash rich, but time poor. Some of them are cash poor, but time rich. By working together in joint ventures you can achieve far more than you could on your own with a lot less effort.

The best way to take advantage of these possibilities is to get to know the other members of the Mastermind and, over time, build relationships with the individuals you want to work with. The online forum is the perfect place to promote joint ventures and opportunities.

7) One to One Personal Success Coaching

To give you even more individual support and accountability, I have trained some of the most successful graduates from previous Mastermind Programmes to be able to give you monthly, private one to one coaching calls. All of the coaches have successfully completed the Mastermind Programme and smashed the £1m of property and £50,000 income targets. Think how much you will be able to achieve with the support of your own property investing coach holding you to account.

8) Two Days Mentoring Support

The final element of the Mastermind Programme is two days of personal property mentoring. This is where one of our successful coaches will visit you in your home town for two whole days to literally walk you through everything you need to do, step by step, to help you achieve your property goals.

Your recommended next steps

I hope that this has given you a brief overview of how the Property Mastermind Programme can help you achieve your property investing goals far more quickly and easily, than if you try to do it on your own.

To find out more about the Property Mastermind Programme and to secure your place on the 'pre-announcement list' for the next available programme, simply visit this website now and register your interest for free:

www.Property-Mastermind.com/Magic

If you are new to investing I recommend that you attend one of my Property Investing Quick Start Seminars. This will give you the opportunity to dip your toe in the water and, see if property investing is right for you and also have the opportunity to see

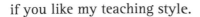

if you like my teaching style.

If you are more experienced and want to learn the advanced strategies, then you should book yourself onto the next 3 day Mastermind Accelerator workshop after which you will absolutely clear, if the full 12 month Property Mastermind Programme is perfect for you.

The Property Mastermind Home Study

And finally, we have just launched my 12 month property Mastermind Home study course which is designed for people who wish to gain the benefits of being on the Mastermind Programme, but cannot physically make it to the advanced Mastermind workshops each month in Birmingham, due to time and or geographical constraints. If that sounds like you, then maybe you should consider our home study programme. Full details here:

www.Property-Mastermind.com/HomeStudy

In conclusion to this chapter, whatever you decide to do in property, remember you are not alone. You don't have to make all the mistakes yourself. You can learn from other people who have already been there, done it and made the mistakes so that you don't have to.

There is now so much information, resources and support available to you that there is no reason why you should not become a successful investor, if that is what you decide to do. I do hope that we will be able to help you further on your property investing journey.

Chapter 9:

A few final words

It's a numbers game

Given that out of every 100 sellers only three or four of them may be motivated enough to give you the kind of deal you are looking for, you need to recognise that this is a numbers game. You will speak to lots of sellers and follow up lots of leads, which may come to nothing. Not every lead you get will turn into a deal; however, every lead you do get is a great opportunity to practise your skills and develop them so that when you get that 'deal of the decade' you are ready to take advantage of it. It would be a real shame to blow your first fantastic deal just because you don't have the experience to handle it. Experience comes with practice, patience and the application of your knowledge. Sometimes knowing where and how to start can be one of the biggest challenges.

Sowing the seeds

Once you have a really good understanding of how you can help motivated sellers, your first job is to set up your lead-generating system. This may be one of the hardest things you have to do as it does require some time and effort to get your systems up and running. Once they are in place they may only need a small amount of maintenance to keep the leads coming through to you.

Many of the lead- generation systems may take some time to start producing results. Some are quicker than others. For example, with a website and use of Google Adwords you could start generating leads instantly, whereas a leaflet campaign may take several weeks to organise and the response may come over a period of several months.

You need to be patient and have faith that as long as you've done the legwork, the leads will come to you. The more seeds you sow, the better results you will receive.

The only reason people fail is because they give up!

Investors, particularly when they are new to investing, get impatient. It is important for you to remember that property investing is a long term investment. One of the great things about property is that you do the work once and you get paid forever! The one slight problem with this is that sometimes you don't get paid straight away. You usually have to wait to enjoy the fruits of your labour.

In today's society, everybody wants instant gratification; they want it all and they want it now. This means if people don't get the results they want in the time they expect, they often think that what they are doing just doesn't work and then they quit. Ironically this is often just before they would have achieved the results they desired, if only they had continued to persevere, rather than giving up.

This idea of giving up seems to be a behaviour we learn as adults. I think most people have a fear of failure (and some have a fear of success). We don't have that fear when we are kids. Did you learn to walk as a child? I am sure that to learn to walk you had to keep trying hundreds, if not thousands, of times to get it right. When it didn't work, did you give up? After months of trying to walk without success, did your parents say to you, "Ah well never mind. You might as well give up. You are never going to be able to walk"? No, of course not. They encouraged you. You kept at it. You persevered, learning from your mistakes and eventually you learned to walk, something which you do now without even thinking about.

At first, property investing may seem like a very daunting task. However, once you know the secret, just like magic, it's actually quite simple. With the correct strategy, some belief, positive action – oh and somebody else's money – you can do it!

I look forward to hearing about your future success.

Best wishes, Simon Zutshi

Notes:

Notes: